# Autc
# Inside and Out

The Best of

## L Y N N  A L L E N

from CADENCE Magazine

**Miller Freeman Books**

San Francisco

Published by Miller Freeman Books
600 Harrison Street
San Francisco, CA 94107

Miller Freeman, Inc. is a United News & Media company
Publishers of CADENCE magazine

Distributed to the book trade in the U.S. and Canada by
Publishers Group West
P.O. Box 8843, Emeryville, CA 94662

ISBN 0-87930-517-7

Cover design by Deborah Chusid
Text design and composition by Brad Greene

Printed in the United States of America
97 98 99 00 01    5 4 3 2 1

To Ashley & Joshua

# TABLE OF CONTENTS

# SECTION 3 The Finale: Taking the Reins of AutoCAD

# PREFACE

Since 1993 I've been writing a monthly column for *CADENCE* magazine about mastering the finer points of AutoCAD, and I frequently get requests for back issues of my column. Well, for all you loyal column readers, here they are, all under one convenient roof. And even if you've never read my column before, this book has a lot of goodies for any AutoCAD user. It is not intended to help you learn AutoCAD from scratch, but to fill in the holes of information and lead you down the road to total productivity. If you need to learn AutoCAD from scratch, then you should take a class (preferably from an Autodesk Training Center). My 12 years in the business of Instructor-Led training forces me to tell you this ... or you can choose to spend ten times as long learning it on your own.

I've done my best to update my articles to reflect the current release of AutoCAD, the wonderful Release 14. You'll still find plenty of references to Release 12 and 13 should you be one of the many who are still on previous releases. This book is not meant to be digested at one sitting, but to be sipped in small doses. Read an article a week, highlight anything new you learn and force yourself to apply it in your everyday AutoCAD life. Being open minded and trying new methods is the only way you'll truly become a CAD guru.

Over the many years I have picked up various AutoCAD tips and tricks and you'll find these embedded in my articles. I have been fortunate enough to work for the Mother company itself, Autodesk. Within the walls of Autodesk I have discovered many amazing AutoCAD facts that have definitely led to more interesting and valuable articles. I thank all who have been kind enough to accompany me on the way as I've explored the caverns of AutoCAD from release to release. For those who know me well, you know that I am truly a cheerleader for AutoCAD. I was before I joined Autodesk, and will continue to be as long as AutoCAD remains the awesome product that it is today.

My new role at Autodesk as User Group Manager enables me to work more closely with AutoCAD users all over the world (that would be you!). I have the privilege of speaking at many User Groups and finding out what's going on in the real world. I would encourage all of you to find your local user group and attend the meetings. I would also encourage you all to join AUGI—Autodesk User Group International. For your convenience I've included an AUGI membership form in the back of the book. If you truly want to hone your AutoCAD skills, AUGI and your local user group will help you meet your goal.

I would like to thanks Kathleen Maher, Roopinder Tara, and George Walsh for their support (and patience) with me for the past 5 years. Had Kathleen not given me this opportunity over five years ago I know I wouldn't be where I am today. Roopinder has stuck by me and George has had the unpleasant job of nagging me every month for my column. Now he's been replaced by Arnie Williams whom I'm sure will do a fine job of filling his shoes.

I would like to thank Marsha Robison who REALLY taught me AutoCAD. She also had the confidence in me to take me under her wing, work with me, and help me become a great AutoCAD instructor. To Ton Bui who gave me free reign at MTI College to manage and teach at the Autodesk Training Center. To Perry Burch who became my protégé, side-kick and good friend. To Jerry Ford from Autodesk whom I idolized for years for his incredible grasp of AutoCAD and his willingness to hire me into the Autodesk training department. A special thanks goes out to Paul Jackson (D.C.) who introduced me to the world of AUGI many years ago. To Don Brown, my beloved arch-enemy who proved to have considerable influence over me and my career. And to James Dyer who has advised and supported me for over two years.

I don't like reading long prefaces, and hence I usually skip over them. With that in mind I will keep this short. This book is dedicated to every single person who has written or told me how much they've enjoyed my column. Hearing this has never gotten old and is always appreciated. It's also dedicated to my two wonderful children, Ashley and Joshua, who have had to share me with the AutoCAD community. They took the brunt of it when I was too busy writing my column to spend time with them. I could never have done it without their love and support.

To all of you,
*Lynn Allen*

P.S. I don't look at all like the picture you've seen every month in *CADENCE*. Just thought you should know.

# Ground Zero: The Simple Stuff

# We're Off to See
# the Wizard!

Setting up the initial drawing environment can be daunting for the new user. Previous releases of AutoCAD have been less than friendly in this department. You had to know what to do and where to go. With AutoCAD R14, this is no longer the case. The new Drawing Setup Wizard will wave its magic wand and make it easy to set up the initial drawing environment. Don't turn your nose up at the Drawing Setup Wizard if you're an AutoCAD veteran—some tricks are included for you as well.

There's no escaping the Wizard when you first load AutoCAD R14. It pops up on the screen when you first boot up AutoCAD as well as whenever you start a new drawing. You can banish the startup Wizard in the Compatibility Tab within the Preferences dialog box (which you select from the Tools menu) or by toggling off the check box in the lower left-hand corner of the Start Up dialog box, as shown in Figure 1.

**Figure 1:** The Start Up dialog box appears when you first launch AutoCAD R14.

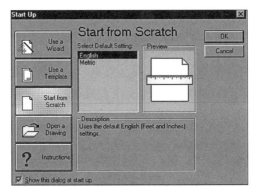

Before sending the Start Up dialog box into exile, I suggest you read further. I'm confident you'll find value within the Wizard! (Note: Although you can tell AutoCAD not to display the Start Up dialog box when you launch AutoCAD, it still displays the dialog box whenever you begin a new drawing.) Let's begin our tour with Instructions.

## Instructions

This selection provides you with a brief explanation of all of the buttons within the dialog box, as shown in Figure 2.

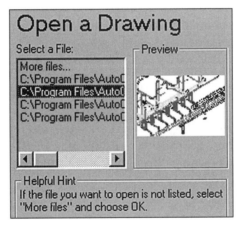

**Instructions**

The buttons on the left determine how you begin a drawing.

Choose "Use a Wizard" to be led through setting up a drawing.

Choose "Use a Template" to start a drawing based on a template.

Choose "Start from Scratch" to begin drawing quickly using default English or metric settings.

Choose "Open a Drawing" to open an existing drawing.

**Figure 2:** Instructions for the Start Up dialog box.

## Open a Drawing

This option only appears when you launch Auto-CAD. You will find the last four drawing files you opened conveniently listed as well as an option entitled More files... that will take you to the standard Files dialog box (Microsoft Foundation Class-compliant

**Open a Drawing**

Select a File:

More files...
C:\Program Files\AutoC
C:\Program Files\AutoC
C:\Program Files\AutoC
C:\Program Files\AutoC

Preview

Helpful Hint
If the file you want to open is not listed, select "More files" and choose OK.

**Figure 3:** The Open a Drawing selection in the Start Up dialog box with a thumbnail preview.

of course). When you single-click on a drawing, you'll also get a thumbnail preview of the drawing, as shown in Figure 3.

## Start from Scratch (the default)

This option works as we've always worked, loading the ACAD template file in the background. You're asked to select between English units (feet and inches) or Metric (a half-step forward).

The icon of the ruler changes as you toggle between English and Metric (nice touch!). Should you banish the Drawing Wizard dialog box with an [Enter], this option is the one AutoCAD will select for you.

## Use a Template

If you're a skilled AutoCAD user, you'll find that this option is a twist on the familiar theme of prototypes. Switching to the universal concept of templates fits nicely with Microsoft standards. New users will find this to be a logical, consistent approach to setting up drawings.

In the past, we used prototypes as our base drawings. We might have many different prototypes for many different disciplines or projects. These files had an extension of DWG, but new template files have an extension of DWT. What's the underlying difference? You guessed it—one letter! Behind the name, they're exactly the same. To accommodate this new mode of thinking, I suggest simply renaming all of your prototype drawings accordingly. I find this to be the simplest approach. You can still select a DWG file as a template—it just requires an extra step (and we dislike extra steps).

You'll notice that AutoCAD R14 comes with an assortment of template files. These are comprised of a variety of different title blocks and borders, each with a nice preview and description. Double-clicking on More files... from the list will take you to a Select Template dialog box listing all of the DWT files in the template directory. You'll find that you can switch the File of Type option to view DWG files instead (that's the extra step).

You'll also find that you can save drawing files as template (DWT) files in the SAVEAS command.

## Use a Wizard

AutoCAD R14 comes with two drawing wizards: Quick Setup and Advanced Setup, as shown in Figure 4. Quick Setup is just a subset of Advanced Setup. The two Quick Setup tabs are Area (previously known as Limits) and Units. We'll explore the entire Advanced Wizard tab by tab.

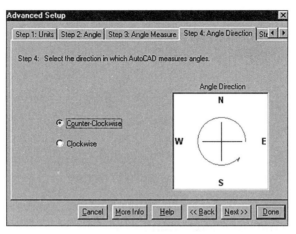

**Figure 4:** Along with a variety of unit measurement styles, Advanced Setup offers five options for specifying angles as well as the precision.

**Step 1: Units.** This option is used to set up the proper drawing units for linear measurement and controls the format for entering and displaying coordinates. Would you like to work in feet and inches, decimals, fractional, or scientific notation? As you select the different options, you'll notice that the image representing the sample units changes as well. You can also control unit precision at this tab. This part replaces the need to use either the UNITS or the DDUNITS command. (Note: The precision selected only controls the display of your drawing units and does not control the accuracy of the drawing.)

**Step 2: Angle.** This tab is used to select the angle display format. You will also need to provide input in the same format you select. Do you work in degrees, minutes and seconds, or perhaps in radians? The sample angle image changes as you select different options. You can also control the precision you'd like your angles to display. This value was set in either the UNITS or the DDUNITS command in previous releases.

**Step 3: Angle Measure.** AutoCAD lets you decide where you'd like angle 0 to be. Most of us are content to leave it at 3:00 (East), but surveyors are the first to move angle 0 to 12:00 (North). This value was also set in the UNITS command in previous releases.

**Step 4: Angle Direction.** It seems to me that Step 3 (assigning angle 0) and Step 4 (direction in which ACAD measures angles) could have been combined into one tab. If you change one, you usually change the other. By default, angles are measured counter clockwise. Some applications prefer the angles to be measured in a clockwise direction.

You'll need to click the right-facing arrow at the top of the dialog box to see the final three tabs. You can also select a tab at a time by clicking the Next>> button.

**Step 5: Area.** Select this option to set up the drawing area. (The LIMITS command was used in previous releases of Auto-CAD to set this same value.) Now this does not mean you'll key in the size of the piece of paper you'll be using but rather the real-world drawing size. In CAD, you draw one-to-one, meaning you draw everything exactly the size it is in real life. If you are drawing a house that is 50' by 40', you want to insure your drawing area, or limits, is set even larger. The drawing area, or limits, also controls the size of the grid display.

You'll notice that, as you set the Width and Length values, the sample area image changes to reflect those values. (Note: As you make changes to the limits of your drawing, you'll notice that AutoCAD also changes the Grid and Snap settings to corresponding values).

**Step 6: Title Block.** This is a great addition, providing easy access to title blocks! Though AutoCAD comes with a few canned title blocks, you can easily add your own. As shown in Figure 5, you can use the up and down arrow keys to see the thumbnail images of the title blocks.

The Add option opens a File dialog box listing DWG files. The Remove option is great for removing title blocks that you'll never use from the canned list.

**Step 7: Layout.** The final tab in the Advanced Setup Wizard serves as a simple introduction to the world of Paper Space, as shown in Figure 6.

The first question is key to being able to use the other options within the dialog box.

Do you want to use advanced Paper Space layout capabilities? If you change

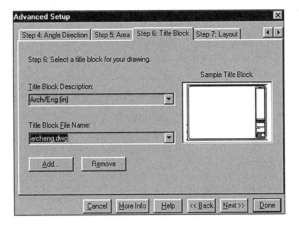

**Figure 5:** The Title Block tab in the Advanced Setup dialog box. Arch/Eng (in) has been selected.

from the default answer of Yes and select No, the other options will gray out and become unavailable. Leaving it set to Yes won't hurt anything. It doesn't automatically zap you into the world of Paper Space.

You can call up a brief explanation of Paper Space by clicking on the What is Paper Space? button. Nice try, but it is very difficult to successfully explain the complex concept of Paper Space in a brief paragraph. (Paper Space was covered in more detail in Circles and Lines, "Lost in Paper Space [Part 1]," September 1996, pp. 71-74 and "Lost in Paper Space [The Sequel]," October 1996, pp.69-74.) You may also notice that the grey text is difficult to read.

The three How Do You Want To Start? options in this tab are somewhat confusing. Let's look closer.

*Work on my drawing while viewing the layout.* Tilemode is set to 0, but you're inside a Model

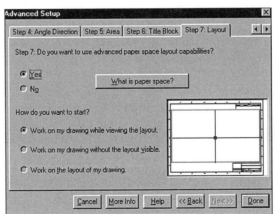

**Figure 6:** The Layout tab serves as a simple introduction to Paper Space.

Space viewport. The title block is placed in Paper Space.

*Work on my drawing without the layout visible.* Tilemode is set to 1 and you're completely working in Model Space. Heads up— your title block is now in Paper Space.

*Work on the layout of my drawing.* Tilemode is set to 0 and you're working in Paper Space. A viewport is available for your model (should you switch back to the world of Model Space). You'll see your selected title block.

So that's the new AutoCAD Drawing Setup Wizard. I'm sure you can see how new users can benefit from this new addition to R14. I believe that the rest of us may have to resist the urge to automatically bypass it and instead try to familiarize ourselves with this new technique for drawing setup.

For those of you who simply can't stand the new Drawing Setup Wizard, I'm including the following lisp routine you can use to make it disappear for good—although I don't condone it!

Lisp Routine:

```
(defun c:new ()
  (setq fdia (getvar "filedia"))
  (setq cecho (getvar "cmdecho"))
  (setvar "cmdecho" 1)
  (setvar "filedia" 0)
  (if (and (> (getvar "dbmod") 0) (= "Drawing.dwg" (getvar
  "dwgname")))
  (progn
  (initget "Yes No")
  (setq ans (getkword "would you like to save the drawing <Yes/No>
  "))
  (if (= ans "Yes")
  (progn
    (command "save" pause)
  (command ".new" "."))
  (command ".new" "Yes" ".")
  )
  )
  )
(if (and (> (getvar "dbmod") 0) (/= "Drawing.dwg" (getvar
  "dwgname")))
  (command ".new" pause ".")
 )
  (if (= (getvar "dbmod") 0)
      (command ".new" ".")
 )
  (setvar "filedia" fdia)
  (setvar "cmdecho" cecho)
)
 (defun S::STARTUP (/ cecho)
 (setq cecho (getvar "cmdecho"))
 (setvar "cmdecho" 0)
 (command "undefine" "new")
(setvar "cmdecho" cecho)
 (princ)
 )
```

# Hidden Treasures
# in the R14
# User Interface

Each time I open a new release of AutoCAD for the first time, I cringe in fear of what might have happened to my beloved AutoCAD screen. I must admit that my greatest fears were realized when I faced AutoCAD R13 for the first time and found myself inundated with toolbars. Though time heals all wounds as one becomes familiar with the new user interface, I prefer not to endure any pain in the first place. And even though menus may not be laid out for maximum efficiency, once I've memorized the command positions, I don't really care. However, it can be frustrating when new releases shuffle the locations of menus and force users to recommit the new locations to memory. Users are typically willing to forgive dramatic changes to the user interface, as long as the changes prove to be worthwhile and going down the road to maximum productivity.

I'm completely convinced that one of the reasons AutoCAD DOS users have been so resistant to upgrading to the Windows environment isn't related to speed—it's because of the user interface. Though the Windows interface can be more pleasant to the eye, the DOS users are completely comfortable in their environment. They know exactly where everything is. One of the nicest things resellers can do for their DOS clients converting over to Windows, is turn off most of the toolbars until they are ready to try them. In fact, the closer the users are to their cozy DOS world, the happier they'll be. Dunking DOS users all at once can cause them to run scared, clutching their R12 DOS box for dear life. I affectionately refer to those who fall into this category (and I've been there myself) as "UI challenged." You know who you are.

The trick to mastering the user interface is to have an open mind with an investigative soul. Forcing yourself to try new things and breaking old habits may prove much more productive in the long run. This month, I'm going to cover the new features that affect the UI in AutoCAD R14 and help you get the most out of them. You'd be surprised how many tasty morsels are hiding in the R14 interface that you'd be hard pressed to find on your own!

On opening R14 for the first time, you'll find a few modifications to the interface right off the bat. You'll see the new Startup Wizard "We're Off to See a Wizard," which has been added to help you set up the proper drawing environment. After banishing the Startup Wizard, you may also find three brand new toolbars—all with the new Bonus Tools. I say "may" find because they only display if you selected the full installation of AutoCAD R14. You'll probably choose to banish the toolbars temporarily as well, since they are likely to be hanging in prime territory on your desktop.

Whether you start a new drawing or open an existing one, you'll find the new Draw and Modify toolbars off to the left of the screen. You'll find them docked, unlike the default floating status in R13. For those of you who frequently used the toolbars in R13, you'll also notice that all of the flyouts in these two toolbars have been removed—all save one (extra credit if you can name which one). The reason behind this fairly drastic change is due to user feedback from R13. Many users complained that the flyouts were just too overwhelming and difficult to learn since they were dynamically updating as you selected different flyouts. From an instructor's standpoint, they were extremely difficult to use for teaching purposes. What the students had on their screen often varied from what the instructor was demonstrating.

So, what about those of you who learned to love the flyouts and actually incorporated them into your daily CAD routine? Well, I'd be lying to you if I told you there was an easy way to get your menu to contain the flyouts it did before. You can create flyouts and add the various tools that suit you, however, through the customization of toolbars. You can also snatch the Draw and Modify toolbars from the AutoCAD R13 menu (*acad.mnu* or *acadfull.mnu*) and put them in the AutoCAD R14 menus if you're familiar with menu structures. Because of the many requests for the return of flyouts, I suspect this issue will definitely be addressed in the near future.

I spoke at a user group not too long ago and was greeted with a couple of hisses when I mentioned the flyouts had been removed (it wasn't pretty). See, even the progressive AutoCAD users can be "UI challenged" to some degree. I never really became comfortable using the many flyouts so it didn't affect me, but if I'd invested the time to do so, I'd also be really grumpy with this modification.

Moving our sights to the bottom of the drawing editor, you'll notice the addition of the *z* coordinate in the status bar (hoorah for 3D!) as well as the new Osnap button. The Osnap button is used to toggle on and off running object snap modes. You still have to double click to toggle these buttons, which conforms to Microsoft standards. You'll find yourself double clicking in Microsoft Word or PowerPoint as well.

Statistics show that just about all AutoCAD users use the pull-down menus; consequently, the way these are laid out is extremely important. Remember how the popular editing commands were broken up between the Construct and Modify pull-down menus in R13? It was so frustrating trying to decide which of the two pull-downs contained the desired command. Well, you'll find these two menus were combined in R14 to form one single Modify menu (Hoorah!).

You'll also find that the toolbars and the pull-down menus are pretty much mapped to each other. This consistency will be very beneficial to the new users as well as those DOS users making the leap to Windows. You'll find some of the R13 flyout options residing within the pull-downs in the form of cascades (for example: the different methods of creating a circle). Many of my favorite cascades have been removed, especially in the Modify menu. Where did the various Break options go, or the Array options? Hopefully, they'll find their way home down the road.

You'll also find that crosshairs have shrunk and now resemble a cursor. If this change is distressing to you, change it back to standard crosshairs in the Preferences dialog box (the Cursor tab). I'll cover this in just a minute.

## Right Click Menus

AutoCAD R14 is filled with a plethora of right-click menus—I absolutely love them. They turn up everywhere, and I look for more to be added in future releases. For starters, note the menu

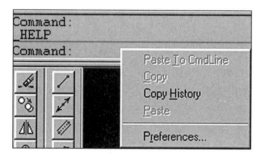

**Figure 1:** Right clicking over the command prompt calls up this menu.

that displays when you right click over the command prompt area, as shown in Figure 1.

I find I use the Preferences option in this right-click menu often. Though I often key in the AutoCAD commands, the PREFERENCES command is just too long for me to deal with. It's within the PREFERENCES command, under the Display tab, that you can set many of your UI options, as shown in Figure 2. Let's take a look.

For those of you DOS die-hards, you can display the Auto-CAD Screen menu on the right-hand side of the drawing editor. Though this menu has been carefully kept and cultivated in the past with essentially all the AutoCAD commands, I think you'll find the Screen menu now simply mimics the pull-down menus. You'll find the familiar four stars of the Screen menu sends you straight to the object snaps (the same layout as the Cursor

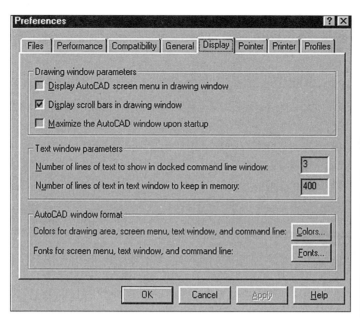

menu), and there's a handy Assist menu comprised of the object selection methods and a couple of other frequently used commands (Did they really feel the GROUP command belongs in here?). Since AutoCAD real estate is typically elongated horizontally anyway, you might well find that the Screen menu, as shown in Figure 3, suits you.

Many of my students rely on the scroll bars across the bottom and side of the drawing window to pan around in the drawing. I've never grown accustomed to them myself and sometimes find them bothersome when I accidentally launch them while creating large crossing windows. I turn mine off, but many of you will choose to leave them on.

Do you want AutoCAD maximized upon startup? How many lines do you want to display within the command prompt area? Three usually suits most people fine. You can also control the number of the lines of text you want AutoCAD to store in memory. The default of 400 may be overkill—valid values are from 25 to 2048.

Within this dialog you can also change the colors and font of the AutoCAD drawing window. I've seen everything from

**Figure 3:** The AutoCAD R14 Screen menu.

**Figure 4:** The cursor size defaults to five percent of the screen.

camouflage to "Miami Vice" colors.

It's within the Preferences dialog box, the Pointer tab, that you can control the size of the cursor. The cursor size is measured relative to a percentage of the screen size. The default is five percent, as shown in Figure 4. Changing the cursor size to 100 will bring back the crosshairs you know and love. I must admit I'm UI challenged in this area, I prefer the crosshairs. The smaller cursor was, however, a huge wish-list request.

So what about the Function keys in AutoCAD R14? If you've used AutoCAD for any length of time, you've come to appreciate the speed in using the various function key settings. Let's take a look at these keys, as shown in Table 1.

Right-click menus also appear in any of the file dialog boxes. Because these dialog boxes are Microsoft Foundation Class-compliant, they support a variety of right-click menus, depending on where you pick. Picking on a filename will give a slightly different menu than picking on a directory. Right clicking on any button will give you "What's this" help information. Figure 5 shows an example of a right-click menu in the OPEN command's Select File dialog box.

Notice what happens when you right-click in the Layer dialog box. You will get a shortcut menu that lets you select or clear all of the layers. My very favorite right-click menu is displayed when you right click on a hot grip (a selected object

**Figure 5:** Right clicking on a folder icon in the OPEN command's Select File dialog box calls up this menu.

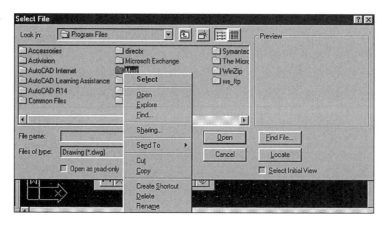

| Table 1. | AutoCAD R14 Function Keys |
| --- | --- |
| [F1] | Help (Windows standard) |
| [F2] | Toggles the text screen |
| [F3] | Toggles on and off running object snaps |
| [F4] | Toggles the tablet calibration on and off |
| [F5] | Toggles from one isometric plane to another |
| [F6] | Toggles the coordinates on and off |
| [F7] | Toggles the Grid on and off |
| [F8] | Toggles the Ortho on and off |
| [F9] | Toggles the Snap on and off |
| [F10] | Toggles the status bar on and off |
| [F11] - [F12] | Nothing (but you can configure them yourself!) |

grip), as shown in Figure 6. You can quickly select the desired grip option or change the properties of the selected objects. You can also go to a URL if there's one associated with the selected object. If you're a grip user, you'll love this added capability.

Of course, right clicking on a toolbar will take you to the Toolbars dialog box, as shown in Figure 7. The new check boxes make it much easier to control the display of the toolbars. I lost plenty of toolbars into space never to return again with R13. The only way to bring them back was to execute the cumbersome TOOLBAR command and enter the cryptic toolbar name. I'm happy to report that I haven't had the same problem with R14.

For further toolbar fun, try right clicking twice on a button, and you'll find that you can customize the toolbar.

One last tidbit of UI information should appeal to all of us who still rely heavily

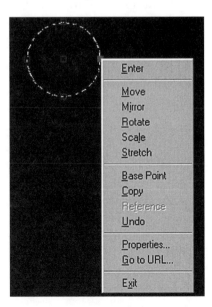

**Figure 6:** The hotgrip right-click menu.

**Figure 7:** The Tool-bar dialog box.

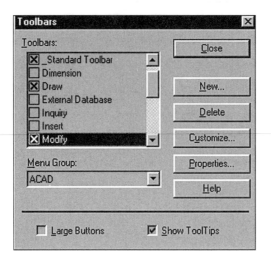

on keyboard entry. AutoCAD has added great functionality to the arrow keys. Do you remember the old DOS key days when you could use [F3] to repeat the last command? Well now the arrow key functions in much the same way. The [3] key stair steps through past commands one at a time. When you get to the command you want, simply execute with an [Enter]. The [4] key steps forward through the command list. If you've ever misspelled a long command or system variable name, you'll love this ability to recall your previously typed line [3]; use the left and right arrows to make the correction. Gotta love it!

Hopefully, this chapter has shown you the benefits in the new AutoCAD R14 User Interface. I'm sure in your CAD adventures you'll find plenty more I haven't touched on (do share!). Sit back, relax and make yourself at home in the new environment—at least until the next release of AutoCAD!

# The World of Object Snaps

Using object snaps is an integral part of AutoCAD. Drawing without them would be tedious, inaccurate, and painful. But are you using them to their fullest potential? Do you truly understand all the object snaps and their complete functionality? Are you just using the ones you think you need?

This chapter will cover each object snap in detail. We'll tour the different methods of grabbing object snaps and their proper implementation. Though object snaps appear to be simple, be sure you're maximizing their usage.

When you're using an object snap (often referred to as "osnap"), you're simply snapping to a specific geometric point on an entity. Object snaps are always accurate and much easier than trying to find the desired point yourself. Object snaps can be used anytime you're asked to indicate a point within your drawing. Osnaps will not grab objects that are not visible or between the dashes of a noncontinuous linetype.

Whether you've learned to grab the object snaps from pull-downs, tablet menus, or toolbars, you've seen the extensive listing of object snaps. You can use object snaps temporarily or set a running object snap mode. Our tour will follow the object snaps as they appear in the cursor pull-down menu. The minimum command-line interface is included in parentheses for those of you who still enjoy typing.

**From (FRO):** First introduced in Release 13, the From object snap definition seems to be missing from the AutoCAD reference guides or help function. From permits users to select a point of reference before selecting their final point. Many of you have used the ID command for this very purpose or moved the UCS for quick reference.The object snap From makes this process much simpler. For example, I might want to insert a door symbol four inches from the corner of a room. From the insertion point option in the INSERT command, I can use the From object snap to select the corner of the room. I follow this up by @4<90 (polar coordinates) and my door snaps right into place. I can use relative or polar coordinates, but I must use the @ sign or AutoCAD will reference absolute coordinates. If you wanted to place a tooling hole two units over and up from an existing part of a drawing, the From object snap would be a good choice.

**Endpoint (ENDP):** Utilized frequently by AutoCAD users, the Endpoint object snap is used to grab the closest endpoints of objects such as lines, arcs, elliptical arcs, mlines, rays, splines, 3D faces, 3D solids, regions, and polylines. EndPoint also snaps to the vertices of polylines (which naturally include polygons, rectangles, and so on). The Endpoint osnap also grabs the closest vertex of such antiquated objects as solids and traces.

The keyboard equivalent to the Endpoint object snap is actually END as opposed to ENDP. However, should you accidentally key in END and find yourself at the command prompt rather then within a command, you may be on your way to exiting AutoCAD. One minute you're looking for an endpoint and the next you're looking at the Windows Program Manager.

**Midpoint (MID):** Grabs the midpoint of a line, arc, polyline segment, spline, elliptical arc, solid (from the SOLID command), region, or bhatch segment. You can't grab the midpoint of a ray despite what the help function and manual claim. Logically, midpoint finds the midpoint of the sides of some 3D solids. If you have given an arc or line an extrusion thickness, you can snap to the midpoint of the extrusion.

**Intersection (INT):** The INTersection object snap is a very popular tool that grabs imaginary or real intersections. By definition, an intersection is where one or more objects cross. An imaginary intersection is where one or more objects would cross if extended in the same direction. Release 13 very generously modified the INT object snap to accept these imaginary extended intersections.

The INT osnap contains one additional modification in it: the ability to select two objects one at a time so AutoCAD can find the intersection. When the osnap aperture doesn't find an actual intersection after the first pick, it will prompt you for another object. This capability is great when its difficult to get into tight places.

Though some of you are Intersection junkies, you should be aware that it takes AutoCAD just a little bit longer to calculate the intersection algorithm and may not be the fastest object snap. When grabbing corners, though INT would work functionally, I strongly recommend the faster and easier Endpoint object snap. The INT object snap is only accurate to a certain degree, for the sake of speed, so I suggest you only use this option when no other object snap will do. If you've ever tried to trim objects that you constructed with INT and were told you couldn't, INT is to blame.

**Apparent Intersection (APPINT):** APPINT is extremely important for 3D users. Also added to Release 13, the Apparent Intersection object snap lets you snap to two objects that intersect in the current viewing plane, though they don't actually meet in 3D space. APPINT works just like the INT object snap, but the objects have to cross or meet in the current viewing plane. APPINT will also graciously extend the objects to an imaginary intersection. The objects can also be selected individually, as in the INT object snap.

**Center (CEN):** CEN is used to snap to the center of an arc, circle, nurbs based ellipses and some 3D solids.

**Quadrant (QUA):** This often forgotten object snap can actually be quite useful. It's used to snap to the nearest quadrant of an arc, circle, ellipse, and some 3D solids. If an arc isn't large enough to have a quadrant, you'll receive an error message.

**Perpendicular (PER):** PER is used to snap to a point perpendicular to the selected object. A reference point is usually selected first. You can snap perpendicular to most 2D geometry and some 3D.

**Tangent (TAN):** The tangent osnap is used to snap to the tangent of an object. Similar to Perpendic-ular, a reference is usually selected first. To create a circle tangent to three lines, you could use the TAN osnap combined with the 3P option in the CIRCLE command. Perpendicular and Tangent won't let you break any rules of geometry.

**Node (NOD):** Used to snap to points created in the POINT command. Points can prove invaluable in the DIVIDE and MEASURE commands, where snapping to them is the next logical step. Be sure PDMODE is set to a decent value (3, for example) to ensure that you can actually see your points. The point style dialog box can be found in the Format pull-down menu.

**Insertion (INS):** This object snap is used to snap to the insertion point of text, a block, or an attribute. You can also snap to the nearly extinct shapes in past releases. This option can be very useful when you want to add another line of text directly below an existing text string while maintaining consistent spacing. Using the DTEXT command, snap to the insertion point of the existing text. When prompted for the new text string, you'll notice the DTEXT box residing on the previous line of text. Hit the space bar (so AutoCAD records something

other than null input)
and hit an extra
<Enter> to drop to the
next line. Your new text
string will line up
directly with the previ-
ous string of text.

**Nearest (NEA):** NEA is
used to snap to the
nearest point of just
about any AutoCAD
object. Nearest doesn't
like text or attributes. It
is defined by the point
closest to the center of
the aperture.

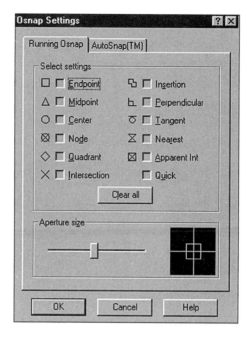

**Figure 1:** The Osnap
Settings dialog box.

**Quick (QUI):** This object snap is quite a chore to explain.
Before Release 12, searching for an object snap point on a large
drawing could be time consuming. Release 11 technology would
comb the entire AutoCAD database from top to bottom searching for the correct object snap value. It searched for all objects
within the aperture, then evaluated them to find the one closest
to the center of the object snap aperture box. AutoCAD wasn't
clever enough to look only within the current display area.
Release 12 changed this process with Oct-tree spatial indexing,
which is just a fancy way of explaining the splitting of the
current display into quadrants for AutoCAD to quickly evaluate
(rather than the entire drawing). Release 12 object searches
were much faster (noticeable only on large drawing files).

Before Release 12, AutoCAD always grabbed the last object
drawn in standard object selection. For those of you who grew
dependent on this fact, Release 12 proved to be frustrating at
first.

Release 11 and previous object snaps could sometimes be
painfully slow. The Quick object snap sometimes proved quite

useful. Quick, combined with one of the other object snap modes, would insist that AutoCAD grab the first qualified object found within the aperture and forget the tedious hunt through *all* objects. The Quick object snap is never used alone but must always be combined with another osnap. This option isn't really necessary in Release 12 or 13. If you are using Release 11 or earlier, I strongly recommend setting the Quick running object snap rather than tediously setting it every time you want to use it. Quick doesn't work with Intersection or APPINT because it still searches through all objects to find the closest intersection.

**None (NON):** Ever have a running object snap that was getting in your way for one or two quick operations? Did you turn your running osnap off completely, then turn it back on when you completed those operations? If so, you're doing too much work. The None object snap turns off the running object snap for one operation only.

When using osnaps, AutoCAD treats polylines and blocks as individual entities. The object snaps do not like blocks that are not uniformly scaled.

We've covered all of the object snap settings. There are two methods of implementing any of these osnaps: temporarily or running. When you pick an osnap from the AutoCAD toolbar (or toolbox in Release 12), the cursor, or tablet menus, you're using temporary object snaps. The desired object snap setting is valid for one step, and then it's gone. This set up permits you to easily use many different object snap settings during one drawing session.

Running object snaps are typically set within the Osnap dialog box (Ddosnap). They can also be set manually with keyboard input in the OSNAP command. The maximum restriction of three running object snap modes has been removed. To turn running object snaps off in the OSNAP command, simply hit an extra <Enter> in the OSNAP command, which will clear all existing object snap settings. Release 14 added an OSNAP button to the status bar which launches the OSNAP dialog box if running object snaps have not been set yet. After that the OSNAP button can be used to turn ON and Off running object snap modes. (See next chapter for more information.)

All the object snaps are available except for From (which is logical). The Ddosnap dialog box also permits easy manipulation of the aperture size with slider bars. You can set multiple running object snap modes. From the dialog box, it's just a matter of selecting those modes you want activated. From the OSNAP command, multiple modes can be selected by separating them with commas, for example, END,NOD,CEN.

Should you be using any release prior to AutoCAD R14, you'll need to know what happens when you set more than one mode? Which mode does AutoCAD look for first? When using running object snap modes, AutoCAD first evaluates the type of object selected. Then, the appropriate mode is matched with the object. Using our example of END,NOD,CEN, if you selected a circle, AutoCAD would obviously assume the Center object snap. A line would use the Endpoint object snap, and a point would use the Node object snap.

If you set similar modes such as Endpoint and Midpoint that work on the same types of objects, Auto-CAD will grab the osnap your selection point is nearest to. If I selected a line near the midpoint, the Midpoint object snap would be used. If I selected an arc near its endpoint, the Endpoint object snap would be used and so on.

This concludes the quick tour of the AutoCAD object snaps. Expand your object snap horizons!

# AutoSnaps!

**M**ost of us select temporary object snap modes one at a time. We may choose to use the Cursor menu ([Shift]+ right click on the mouse) or the toolbar. We may even still key the modes in at the command prompt. Most of us don't take advantage of setting running object snaps for two reasons: They're too cumbersome to turn on and off, and it's too hard to tell which object snap mode it's using at any given time. You'll find that both of these obstructions to running osnaps have been eliminated with AutoCAD R14.

We welcome the new Osnap button to the status bar. When a running object snap mode is set, double clicking on the Osnap button will toggle the running object snap modes on and off. It can even be used transparently within a command. For those of you who don't care for the Status bar, the function key [F3] will give you the same results.

Double clicking on the Osnap button for the first time (before running object snaps have been set) will send you into the Osnap Settings dialog box, as shown in Figure 1. This dialog box is very similar to the Ddosnap dialog box in previous releases. You will probably notice two major differences: the AutoSnaps tab and the new graphic symbols next to each object snap setting. It will take you awhile before you're familiar enough with each symbol to know which object snap it represents.

Notice that the poor Quick osnap was neglected and didn't get its own symbol (which makes perfect sense). Do any of you still use the Quick object snap? Do any of you even remember what the Quick object snap is for? That's truly a good AutoCAD trivia question. There's not much point in using it anymore now that AutoCAD can search so quickly through its data (there's a small hint).

The main goal behind setting running object snaps is to set up one or more defaults that AutoCAD will automatically find. For example, in dimensioning, it's handy to set a running object snap mode of endpoint. In previous releases of AutoCAD, you wouldn't catch me setting several running object snaps at one time. Setting too many would just confuse me as to which object snap mode AutoCAD is grabbing at any given time, especially when selecting object snaps that relate to the same type of object, such as Center and Quadrant. Because we now have graphical representation of the object snaps, it's no longer an issue—I have a minimum of four set at all times.

As you enter a drawing command, you'll see the object snaps automatically appear on your drawing. The symbol indicates which object snap AutoCAD is using. If you aren't sure which symbol indicates which object snap, holding the cursor still for a moment will display a tooltip, as shown in Figure 2.

You can still override running object snaps by selecting an object snap manually. And if they get in your way, it's easy to toggle them on and off. Let's take a look at the AutoSnaps tab in the Osnap Settings dialog box, as shown in Figure 3. If you decide you don't care for AutoSnaps—you can toggle them off by selecting the marker option (but why?). You'll also find that the AutoSnaps have that same magnetic quality that grips have. When Magnet is on, it locks your cursor onto the snap point. If you don't care for that feature, you can toggle that off as well. After you've progressed to the point where you can identify each of the markers, you may choose to turn off the snap tips if they're bugging you.

**Figure 2:** An AutoSnap tooltip.

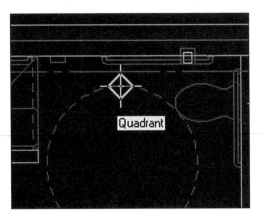

**Figure 3:** The Auto-Snaps tab in the Osnap Setting dialog box.

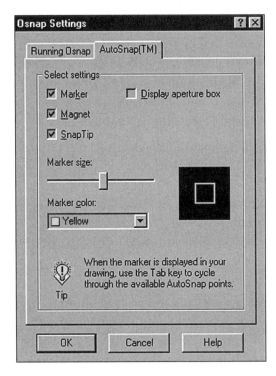

I would expect (and hope) you would leave all of those toggles on and give AutoSnaps a chance. Should you choose to resort back to standard R12 or R13 object snaps, be sure to turn on the Display Aperture Box check box.

The AutoSnaps tab also allows you to control the size and color of the markers. If I had a drawing filled with yellow objects, it might be easier for me to seethe AutoSnaps if they were changed to another color.

You'll notice a hot tip in the AutoSnaps tab. If you find yourself in a position where AutoCAD isn't grabbing the object snap you need, you can use the [Tab] key to cycle through all of the object snaps set for that particular object. This process is very important should you choose Quadrant and Center. AutoCAD will just about always find only the Quadrant object snaps—only the [Tab] key will force it to find the Center object snap.

You can easily get to the Osnap Settings dialog box by selecting the last option in the Cursor menu, as shown in Figure 4. It is also the last option in the Object Snaps buttons in the Standard toolbar. For you who are pull-down menu fans—you'll find it in the Tools menu. Those of you who choose to use the OSNAP command will find that it now launches the dialog box. To use the command-line interface OSNAP command, simply put a dash in front of the command (-OSNAP). For setting a single running object snap mode, the command-line interface is probably still the fastest method.

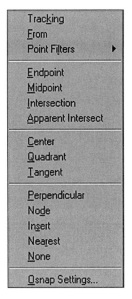

**Figure 4:** Selecting the last item in the Cursor Menu takes you to the Osnap Setting dialog box.

## Tracking: A New Feature

I'd also like to introduce you to an entirely new feature called Tracking. Because Tracking has made its way to the top of the Cursor menu as well as the Osnaps fly-out, I decided it fell under the object snap category. Besides, with its prominent position, it must be important! Tracking is simply another method of locating a position in your drawing. Consider it a combination of the new From object snap that came out in R13 and the .X and .Y filters. When combined with Direct Distance, it becomes *very* powerful! Let's take a look at a couple of examples.

I need to insert a bolt into a front view that aligns with the top view, which means I'll need to use the x coordinate of the corresponding bolt in the top view, as shown in Figure 5. Using Tracking, I can snap to the top view bolt and drag the bolt into position.

Stepping through the process, I would start by executing the INSERT or DDINSERT command. To turn Tracking on, you can key in tk (or select Tracking from the Cursor or Toolbar menu).

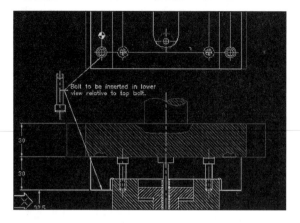

```
Command: INSERT [Enter]
Block name (or ?): BOLT [Enter]
 Insertion point: tk [Enter]
First tracking point: cen [Enter]
of
```

Select the bolt from the top view.

```
Next point  (Press ENTER to end tracking): per [Enter]
to
```

Select the desired location in the lower view.

```
Next point  (Press ENTER to end tracking):  [Enter]
X scale factor <1> / Corner / XYZ: [Enter]
 Y scale factor (default=X): [Enter]
 Rotation angle <0>: [Enter]
```

When prompted for the insertion point, I enter tk to start
tracking. I use the center of the bolt from the top view as my
alignment and drag the bolt down into position. When the bolt
is at its desired location, I lock it in with the final [Enter].

Let's say I need to draw a circle in the center of a rectangle.
Previously, I would have used .X and .Y filters for this, or I
might have drawn a construction line. Tracking can be used
here, as shown in Figure 6:

```
Command: C [Enter]
CIRCLE 3P/2P/TTR/<Center point>: tk [Enter]
```

```
First tracking point: mid [Enter]
of
```

Snap to midpoint of one of the horizontal sides.

```
Next point (Press ENTER to end tracking): mid [Enter]
of
```

Snap to the midpoint of one of the vertical sides.

```
Next point (Press ENTER to end tracking):  [Enter]
Diameter/<Radius>:
```

Tracking is a difficult thing to explain. You really need to practice implementing it yourself (and I encourage you to do so). Remember the following two items about tracking: Tracking locks onto the *x* and *y* coordinates and permits orthog-

onal movement in those two directions only, and you must hit a final [Enter] to turn Tracking back off (when you've finally found your destination point).

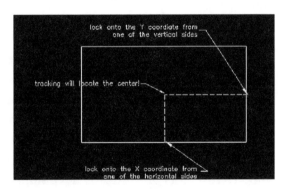

**Figure 6:** Using Tracking to find the center of a rectangle.

# Object
# Selection

AutoCAD is always prompting us to select objects. If you're an experienced user of AutoCAD much of your selection repertoire consists of Crossing, Window, and picking the objects one at a time. Release 12 introduced even more object selection options, but fundamental as they may be, these new options are typically overlooked. We'll take a look at all the possible methods of selecting objects, including the DDS-ELECT dialog box. You'll have an option for every occasion!

Implied windowing came into play with Release 12 (as long as the system variable PICKAUTO is set to 1). Surely by now you veteran users of AutoCAD have stopped keying in C or W for Crossing and Window respectively. By picking the opposite corners of your window in the proper order you can automatically denote Crossing or Window. Picking the two corners from left to right denotes a regular Window. Picking the two corners from right to left denotes a Crossing Window, as shown in Figure 1.

For those of you new to AutoCAD, let me explain a little further. A standard Window will only select those objects completely encompassed by the window (none can remain outside the box). A Crossing Window will select all objects completely encompassed, as well as those that touch (or cross) the window (even if only a minor part of the object lies within the box).

Until Release 12, all windows used in the selection process were rectangular. This setup was fine as long as the objects you wanted to select were cooperative enough to lie in a rectangular region. Because objects are frequently uncooperative, we were often forced to use multiple windows to get the desired selection. Now we can use Polygon Windows, a new type of window that permits windows with more than four sides. You can constrain the polygon windows to any shape with just one rule: the polygon segments cannot cross

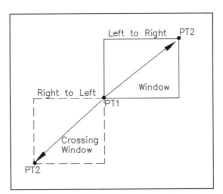

**Figure 1:** Window Selections.

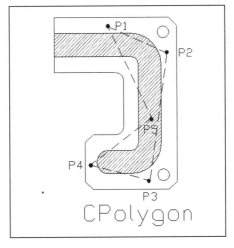

**Figure 2:** Crossing Polygon.

over themselves (like a bowtie). You may create Crossing Polygons (CP), as shown in Figure 2, or Window Polygons (WP). The same rules apply as those previously described, with standard crossing and window options. (Note that CP is also accepted by the Stretch command.)

I completely believe the next option was designed specifically with the Trim command in mind. A standard complaint regarding Trim has been its requirement that objects to be trimmed are selected one at a time. Window selection was not accepted, resulting in very tedious trimming. This problem occurred because windows cannot indicate to AutoCAD which side of the object is to be trimmed. The new Fence option, however, is wholeheartedly accepted by the Trim command, permitting multiple selection.

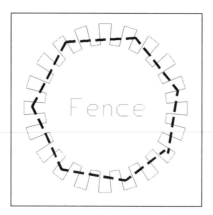

The Fence option, shown in Figure 3, draws a series of connected vectors through the objects you wish to select (resembling a line). There is no need to close these vectors because you're not creating a window. All the objects the Fence passes through will be selected.

Last and Previous are old standbys that deserve mention. Last selects the last object drawn (visible on the screen). If you insert a Block, then promptly decide to move it—try keying in L in response to the Select Objects: prompt. It's a quick and efficient method. Don't forget this option when writing script files or menus that manipulate objects.

The Previous option comes in handy when you wish to manipulate the same group of objects over and over again. First you move the objects, then decide to rotate them. You then realize the objects are on the wrong layer, so you need to change them, and so on. The Previous option reselects your last selection set. Enter a P when prompted to select objects. (Previous won't work after an Erase or an Undo. Previous is also cleared if you switch from Paper Space to Model Space or vice versa.)

By far the most violent of the means of object selection is ALL. ALL (you must key in all three characters as a safety precaution) selects all objects displayed or otherwise. The only objects that remain safe are those on frozen or locked layers. Even those objects on layers that are turned off are not protected from this option. Note that the AutoCAD Reference Manual claims that frozen and locked objects will be selected—definitely not true.

The Multiple option is outdated (and will no doubt eventually disappear). Individual picking of objects scans the drawing immediately after each pick. This could be time consuming on large drawings in earlier releases. The Multiple option allows many picks before scanning the drawing. You end the picking process when you hit <Enter>, which causes a final scan and highlights the selected objects. On the positive side—if you select two objects perfectly transposed upon each other by picking twice, the Multiple option will select both objects, whereas individual picking will not. If you select two objects at an intersection point twice, both objects will be selected—nice trick! The negatives far outweigh the positives, however. The objects don't highlight as you select them (you just hope you're a good shot) and you must key in M to choose the Multiple option. We're programmed for immediate feedback—we expect highlighting. With the increased speed of object selection, the time issue is nearly incidental anyway. Chances are you accidentally encountered the Multiple option in the Copy command by entering M (thinking you were specifying multiple copies) at the Select Objects: prompt. You were a bit premature.

There are two ways to deselect objects after the fact. Let's say you want to erase multiple objects in a region but there are a couple of objects you don't wish to include. Before Release 12 you would use the Remove option to dehighlight those objects you didn't want included in the final selection set. Now the shift key has been brought into the picture, to make this process much simpler. Holding down the shift key while selecting objects will remove them from the selection set, which is a great time-saver. You can even do implied windowing with the shift key down to remove many objects from a selection set.

If you were a bad shot and wish to deselect the last object or group of objects you selected, using the Undo option while in the Select objects mode (not the U command, which is issued at the command prompt) gives you another chance.

Auto and Box (no abbreviation) are used in menu creation and are not keyed in. If you're using Release 12 or higher you won't need these options anyway as implied windowing is available without them.

To review the options:

- Picking one at a time (default)
- Window and Crossing (determined by the order of the selected corners).
- CP—Crossing Polygon
- WP—Window Polygon
- F—Fence
- L—Last
- P—Previous
- M—Multiple (ugh)
- U—Undo
- ALL

Release 12 added four new variables that have some control over our object selection. Let's tackle them one at a time.

## Pickauto

If Pickauto is on, implied windowing is on (as mentioned earlier). Should you inadvertently turn this system variable off, you won't have that great automatic windowing capability. If you pick a vacant point on the screen and AutoCAD doesn't jump into a Window mode, check to ensure that Pickauto is set to 1 (for on).

## Pickdrag

I believe that Pickdrag was added for the Macintosh users of the world. When you select two corners of a window in AutoCAD, you pick with the pick button, remove your finger while moving over to the opposite corner of the window, and pick again. Macintosh users have grown accustomed to holding down the pick button, dragging the window across the screen to the opposite corner, then removing their finger. If you've used any of the Windows paint programs you're quite familiar with this technique as well. You can try this approach to windowing if you turn Pickdrag to 1, but more importantly, if this feature is turned on without your knowledge, you can think your implied windowing isn't working. You'll pick once, move your cursor to the opposite corner, and at that time notice that no window is appearing. If implied windowing isn't working, check this system variable as well.

## Pickfirst

AutoCAD permits you to select objects for editing before entering the desired editing command. For example, at the command prompt, I can pick some objects to erase and then enter the Erase command. AutoCAD assumes the selected objects are the objects to be erased, I'm not permitted to select any more objects, and the objects I've previously selected are erased.

You may have encountered this technique inadvertently. Many CAD users do not like this new feature and turn it off. If you're a heavy grip user this feature can be frustrating. With grips on an object, you enter an editing command with the intention of editing an entirely different group of objects. No such luck—AutoCAD selects the objects with the grips. Turning Pickfirst to 0 (off) will disable this function if you prefer. When Pickfirst is on, the cursor has a target box at the intersection.

Not every one of the AutoCAD editing commands are affected by this setting.

## Pickadd

When Pickadd is disabled, you get only one chance to select a group of objects. If you miss some objects, you can add to the selection set by using the Shift key to select additional objects. Turn Pickadd to 0 and notice the limitations of object selection. Having this setting turned off can be very frustrating.

AutoCAD has a dialog box to help you control these variables. Under the Tools pull-down menu select Object Selection, as shown in Figure 4.

To explain the different options:

- Noun/Verb Selection: Pickfirst
- Use Shift to Add: Pickadd
- Press and Drag: Pickdrag
- Implied Windowing: Pickauto

**Figure 4:** AutoCAD has several different options available under Object Selection to help you control the limitations that occur when Pickadd is disabled.

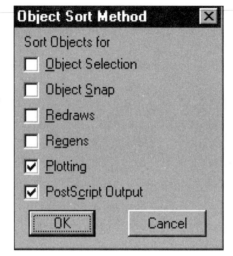

This dialog box also permits controlling the size of the pickbox (the target box) and the method AutoCAD uses to sort it's objects.

Select the Object Sort Method button. You'll see the dialog box shown in Figure 5.

AutoCAD Release 11 and earlier sorted its objects in the order they were created. If you had two objects lying on top of each other and selected only one to erase, AutoCAD would always select the last object you drew. Veteran users of AutoCAD became accustomed to this and used it to their advantage.

Sorting objects in the order created also proved to be slow. AutoCAD wouldn't just sort the objects displayed—it would sort all the objects in the drawing (except those on frozen layers). Large drawings became slow and cumbersome for this very reason.

Using a different technique called Oct-tree spatial indexing, AutoCAD can redraw, regenerate, and select objects faster. AutoCAD can now concentrate on the objects displayed rather than all the objects.

Many pre-Release 12 users have complained about this minor change. If you wish to return to the older method of object selection (and slow yourself down), this dialog box is for you.

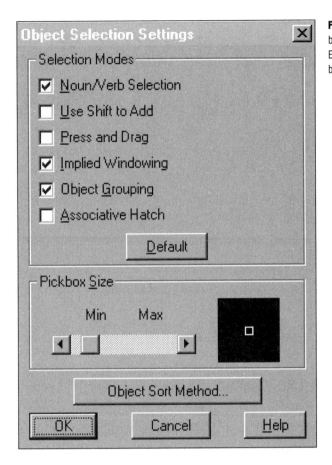

**Figure 5:** This dialog box appears when the Entity Sort Method button is selected.

Use the Object Sort dialog box to select those procedures you wish to sort in the order the objects were created. For example, I want AutoCAD to regenerate the screen starting with the first object I drew to the last. I would select the Regens checkbox. I would also pack a lunch, as this would dramatically slow me down in the case of larger drawings. AutoCAD would now be forced to consider the entire data base of objects. I suspect the only box you would consider selecting would be the Object Selection box.

Hopefully these new object-selection techniques will enhance your AutoCAD productivity. Be adventurous and experiment with some of these new options.

# Layering with AutoCAD R14

S tatistics show that the LAYER command is the second most frequently used command in AutoCAD—second only to the UNDO command (I guess no one is perfect). Everyone who upgrades will run into the new LAYER dialog box right off the bat; there's no escaping it. Besides, the new LAYER dialog box is filled with lots of delicious improvements I'd love to share.

DDLMODES is gone, and the LAYER command is here to stay! That should get your attention. Yes, you can still execute the cumbersome command name of DDLMODES, but you'll find that the age-old LAYER command will take you to the exact same place: the new LAYER dialog box. Here's another tidbit of information: the LINETYPE command will send you to the same dialog box also. You'll find that many of the commands that executed command line interface (CLI) commands have been modified to execute their corresponding dialog box instead. Autodesk is trying to wander away from the DD world. Not many users would opt for a CLI command when they can use a dialog box in its place. Relax, you power-users who still insist there's nothing faster than driving AutoCAD via the command line, you can still access your favorite commands without using the dialog box by putting a dash in front of the desired command. For example, -LAYER will execute the CLI of the LAYER command we've used for more than 10 years. The same

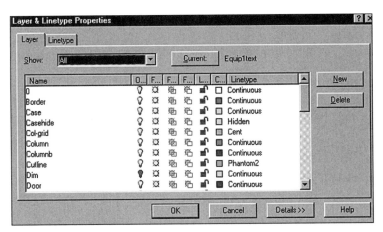

**Figure 1:** The new Layer dialog box.

is true of other commands, including -MTEXT, -OSNAP, and -BHATCH. This information is also crucial for those of you who are master customizers.

Let's take a look at one of AutoCAD's newest masterpieces, shown in Figure 1. Because the Layer and Linetype Properties dialog box is MFC-compliant, you get to enjoy all of the explorer-like qualities you've come to know in Windows 95. You can resize the columns, click on the column headers, display them in ascending and descending order, and so on. I like being able to click on the On/Off column header to quickly display layers that are off and to quickly sort my layers by color. You may notice that the Set Color and Set Linetype buttons are missing. That's because now you can click directly on the color box to go to the Select Color dialog box. This same functionality applies to the Linetype column. So, how do we go about creating new layers?

The New button is still used to add one or more layers to your drawing. For one layer, you simply key in the layer name, followed by an [Enter] to terminate. If you don't key in a name, AutoCAD will create a new layer called Layer1. Each time you hit the New button, AutoCAD will add another layer and supply the default layer name in numbered increments (Layer2, Layer3, and so forth). To create multiple layers at one time, separate the layer names by commas, just as we've done in the past. As soon as AutoCAD sees the comma, it will bring you down to the next line and allow you to input another layer name.

The new Delete button has been on users' wish lists for years. Now, AutoCAD allows you to delete unused layers directly from the Layer dialog box (rather than the finicky PURGE command). The key word here is "unused." Referenced layers or layers with objects on them still cannot be deleted.

Two buttons that you may also notice are missing are the Select All and Clear All buttons. A right click within the dialog box will display a simple cursor menu with those two options in it, as shown in Figure 2. Because this may not be obvious to users in the beginning (someone had to show me), AutoCAD provides a friendly reminder in the form of a tool tip.

Selecting the Details button in the lower-right-hand corner will pull down the dialog box, as shown in Figure 3.

The Layer Details dialog box can also be used to modify specific settings for a particular layer. Because you can achieve the same goal in the main dialog box, I don't find this capability too intriguing. I do, however, like the check box in the lower-left-hand corner that reads "Retain changes to xref-dependent

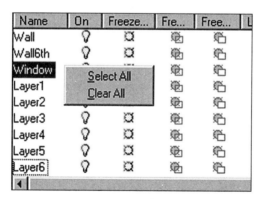

**Figure 2:** The right-click cursor menu.

**Figure 3:** The Layer Details dialog box.

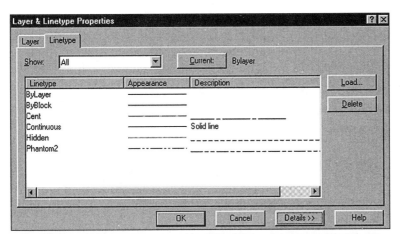

**Figure 4:** The Linetype dialog box.

**Figure 5:** The Linetype Details dialog box.

layer." No longer do you need to use the visretain system variable. This check box will remember any layer settings you've set for xrefed drawings and will retain them for future drawing sessions.ˈ

So, is it clear to you that the only way to close this dialog box once you've opened it is to reselect the Details button? I picked all sorts of buttons before I figured that out. I hope this will be more obvious to others than it was to me.

The new Layer dialog box has two tabs. Let's look at the Linetype tab, as shown in Figure 4. This dialog box is similar to the one in R13. Of course, the Linetype Delete button is new. The Delete button makes it easy to purge unreferenced linetypes from your drawing (using the same idea as the one in the main dialog box). Let's look at the Details button in this dialog box, as shown in Figure 5.

All of the various linetype scale factors are hidden within this dialog box. You have control over the global (LTSCALE) and

**Figure 6:** The Filter drop-down list.

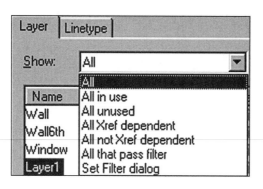

current object scale factors (CELTSCALE). You can also toggle on the linetype scaling for Paper Space viewports (PSLTSCALE). Don't forget, the only way to close this dialog box is to reselect the Details button. Last but not least, let's look at the new Display Filters, shown in Figure 6.

By default, AutoCAD displays all of the layers you create. AutoCAD R14 has added some nice predefined filters to help you control the list of layers within the Layer dialog box. Let's review each filter:

- All in use: Displays all of the referenced layers within your drawing.
- All unused: Displays all of the unreferenced layers—perfect for deleting!
- All xref-dependent: Displays all those layers that belong to an externally referenced drawing.
- All not xref-dependent: Displays only those layers that do not belong to any externally referenced drawings.
- All that pass filter: Displays only those layers that pass the filter test set within the Filter dialog box.
- Set Filter dialog box: Sends you to the new Filter dialog box, shown in Figure 7.

I suppose describing this dialog box as new is exaggerating a bit. There's really only one new feature in this dialog box: the checkbox at the bottom that says "Apply this filter to the layer control on the Object Properties toolbar."

Until R14, we could only control the layer list within the Layer dialog box. The layer ribbon on the Object Property toolbar displayed all of the layers regardless of any set layer filters. Autodesk received many requests to add the capability to apply these filters to both if desired.

Of course, the Filter dialog box lets you filter by name, color, linetype, frozen state, and so on. I did get somewhat annoyed when I set my display back to Show All and my layer ribbon didn't update. Apparently,

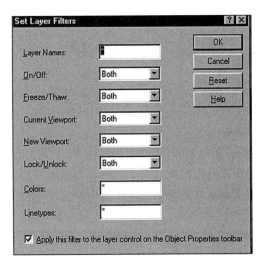

**Figure 7:** The Filter dialog box.

you need to reenter the Layer Filter dialog box and uncheck the box, or the filters will continue to apply to the layer ribbon.

I believe we've tackled everything within the new and improved Layer dialog box, but I'd be remiss if I didn't mention one more tool related to setting layers: the new Make Object's Layer Current button. This new button is the very first tool on the Object Properties toolbar.

The Make Object's Layer Current button implements a handy routine that LISP coders have been using forever. If you've ever wanted to set your current layer to be the same as a particular object on your drawing, but you weren't sure what layer that was, you'll appreciate this new addition. Given this scenario, you'd have to LIST the object in question, then set the current layer accordingly. Our new tool does all of this for you. You select the object, and it does the research and sets a new current layer. Let's look at the command line prompts:

```
Command: (pick the Make Object's Layer Current button)
Select object whose layer will become current: pick the
  object
DIM2 is now the current layer.
```

It's that simple—only two picks.

# Construction Commands

Those of you with a hand-drafting background probably remember drawing countless construction lines as part of your routine drawing practice. Switching over to CAD doesn't necessarily mean those days are over. We'll cover an assortment of construction commands, some that are new and some that are well-hidden old favorites. Many of the commands we'll address are valuable secrets used by a slim percentage of the AutoCAD world.

## Construction Lines

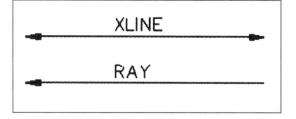

**Figure 1:** An xline Is essentially a line that extends infinitely in both directions. A ray has a starting point and extends infinitely in only one direction.

Two objects were added to AutoCAD in Release 13: xlines and rays, as shown in Figure 1. An xline is a line that extends infinitely in both directions. A ray has a starting point and extends infinitely in only one direction. You may immediately fear the consequence of zooming or plotting to the extents of a drawing, but don't worry. Neither one of these two new objects affect the drawing limits or extents of a drawing. Xlines and rays can be moved, rotated, offset, and so on.

Trimming off half of an xline would leave you with a ray. Trimming off the other half would leave you with a plain old line. If you're going to be using xlines or rays specifically for construction purposes, you might choose to place them on their own layer, which allows you to remove the objects from the screen by freezing the layer. Let's take a look at the two commands in more detail. Both the XLINE and RAY commands are in the Draw pull-down menu. The menu option for xlines is Construction Line.

```
Command: XLINE
Hor/Ver/Ang/Bisect
   /Offset/<From point>:
Through point:
```

The default option, From Point, requests a root for the intended xline. This point becomes the conceptual midpoint of the construction line. Because the object extends infinitely in both directions, it can't have a real midpoint. This root point will also be one of the three object grips assigned to the xline. After placing the root, you will be prompted for a through point. This through point will indicate the direction for the xline. You can create as many xlines as needed within the same command, but they'll all use the same root point.

- **Hor:** Creates horizontal xlines only (parallel to the $x$ axis of the current UCS). You'll be reprompted for each new root point.
- **Ver:** Is the same as Horizontal but the xlines are drawn parallel to the $y$ axis of the current UCS.
- **Angle:** The Angle option allows you to specify an angle or reference an existing object (similar to the ROTATE command):

```
Reference/<Enter angle
   (0)>: r
Select a line object:
Enter angle <0>: 45
Through point:
```

45

By default, you only enter the desired angle of the xlines. You can draw many xlines with different root points, but they will all use the indicated angle.

If you'd prefer to reference an existing object and specify an angle from that object, select the Reference option (see the format in the description of the Angle option).

**Bisect:** Here's one you don't see everyday! The Bisect option is used to create a construction line that bisects a selected angle. You will need to specify three points: the vertex and two points (typically on the lines) that create the angle, as shown in Figure 2.

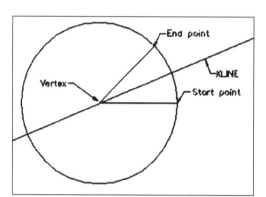

**Figure 2:** The Bisect option is used to create a construction line that bisects a selected angle.

## Offset

Based on the same concept as the OFFSET command, the Offset option in the XLINE command creates a construction line parallel to an existing object. The existing object can be a line, polyline, ray, or another xline. After specifying an offset distance or a through point, you'll be prompted for the object from which you want to offset. Any eligible object has two sides, so specify the side to offset.

A slick use of xlines is used in relation to the new spline object. Create a spline, enter the XLINE command, and specify the Perpendicular object snap. After selecting the spline, you'll see that AutoCAD lets you trace the xline across the spline, keeping it tangent all the while. This method works with other objects but is especially powerful in relation to splines.

## Rays

The RAY command is more limited in scope and options than XLINE. I've only seen a couple of real-world situations where I might use the RAY command while drafting. Projecting center lines up or down in a profile might be a situation where the RAY command would come in handy. The obvious reason to me for creating a ray is to ensure that AutoCAD knows what to generate when you trim off half of an xline.

```
Command: RAY
From point:
Through point:
Through point:
```

You'll notice that you are not given the wide range of options available in the XLINE command. You select a root point and the direction you want the ray to be drawn in.

On a humorous note, the AutoCAD HELP function defines a ray as a "Semi-infinite line." Isn't that akin to being kind-of pregnant?

## Divide and Measure

You AutoCAD Release 12 (and before) users can wake up now. The next two commands have been around for ages but are incredibly underused as powerful construction tools. Without proper understanding of these two commands, a user will see them as useless.

Both DIVIDE and MEASURE have the same fundamental goal: to place markers at even increments along an object. They're great for quickly creating title blocks, placing effects evenly along another object, and so on. To effectively explore these two commands, you'll need a couple of objects to work on; lines and circles will do.

By default, both of the commands use points as markers. If you don't change the Point Display mode to something visible, you'll think DIVIDE, and MEASURE are a waste of time. Remember, by default, points display as minuscule dots, so you won't see them. For Release 14, the point style dialog box is located in the Format pull-down menu. If you prefer to type, the DDP-TYPE command will also call this dialog box. In

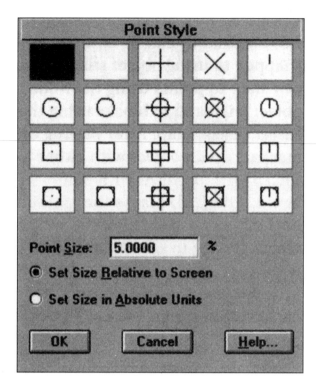

Release 12, the dialog box is located under the Settings menu. Now, select a different point type—the X works well. If you insist on typing or customizing, setting the PDMODE to three will also change the Point style to the X.

The DIVIDE command takes the selected object and divides it into the indicated number of equal sections using markers. The object isn't physically broken. Both DIVIDE and MEASURE can be found in the pulldowns (Release 13 and 14) under DRAW>POINT>. Release 12 has these two commands placed under the Construct pulldown.

```
Command: DIVIDE
Select object to divide:
<Number of segments>/BLock: 5
```

This sequence will divide the selected object into five, equal segments. The range of segments must be between 2 and 32,767. If the object selected was a circle, AutoCAD begins at angle zero and divides in a counterclockwise direction. Closed polylines have a marker placed at the initial starting vertex. If you'd rather place a library symbol (block) than a point as markers, select the Block option in the DIVIDE command.

```
<Number of segments>
/Block: b
Block name to insert:
   tooling_hole
Align block with object?
   <Y>
Number of segments: 3
```

The DIVIDE command only reads block names currently defined within your drawing. If you plan on using a wblock or another drawing name, you'll have to separately insert it first to store the block definition within the drawing. Aligning the block will place the block tangent to or collinear with the selected object. Choosing No will place the blocks along the object at their normal orientation. Figure 4 shows a block of an arc placed on a spline curve.

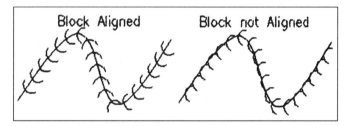

**Figure 4:** A block of an arc placed on a spline curve.

The MEASURE command is similar to the DIVIDE command, because, rather than indicating the number of segments, it's indicating the length of the segments. Auto-CAD divides the selected object into as many segments as is possible, and it is not at all uncommon to have a little extra left over.

```
Command: MEASURE
Select object to measure:
<Segment length>/Block: 1.5
```

The segment length can be keyed in or visually shown by picking two points on the screen. On open objects, AutoCAD will start measuring relative to where you selected the object (so be aware of your pick point). Circles are measured relative to the current angle 0 setting (typically 3:00). The MEASURE command uses radical segments (not chord lengths) when handling arcs or circles.

The markers placed with these two commands can be easily snapped to using object snaps. You can snap to points using the Node object snap and to blocks using the Insert object snap. After placing the markers on an object with either the DIVIDE or MEASURE command, AutoCAD places the markers in the Previous selection set, which makes it easy to select them for editing.

If you are taking the AutoCAD certification exam, I strongly recommend delving into DIVIDE and MEASURE. These two commands are great speed enhancers and will help you race through the drawing portion of the exam.

Other quick construction methods might include the FROM object snap or the ID command for those of you still using Release 12. The ID command lets you select a new @ reference point that you can use in the following draw command. For example, I might want to place a tooling hole one inch up and over from the lower-left-hand corner of a mounting bracket. When prompted for the center of the tooling hole, I would key in **@1,1**. AutoCAD would use the reference point selected in the ID command.

The FROM object snap provides the same functionality but is accessible from within the actual drawing or editing commands. In the same situation, I would forgo the ID command and directly enter the CIRCLE command. When prompted for the center of the hole, I would use the From object snap:

```
Command: CIRCLE
3P/2P/TTR/<Center point>:
from
Base point: end
of <Offset>: @1,1
Diameter/<Radius> <0.9351>:.2
```

The From object snap doesn't like some commands, such as the INSERT command. Being able to quickly construct drawings from scratch is the role of many AutoCAD operators. Time is always an issue, so it's important to know as many short cuts as possible.

# More to Offer
# with Multilines

Multilines (mlines) were added in Release 13 to make
it easy to create a series of parallel lines. Though
mlines were obviously created with the AEC world
in mind, I've seen them used quite creatively in other disciplines. Obvious applications that come to mind are roadways,
electrical, piping, HVAC, and of course, architecture. We'll tour
the innermost sanctum of the new multiline objects and the key
commands associated with them.

The MLINE command is a step up from the Release 12 DLINE
LISP routine. Unlike DLINE, multilines are not limited to a
single linetype and color. The MLINE command can create up to
16 parallel lines at the same time. Each line of an mline is called
an element. You have control of the distance between each element, as well as its color and linetype. In addition to defining
each individual element, you have many options that relate to
the multiline as a whole. Some of these options include capping, filling, and displaying the miter joints.

The three commands directly associated with multilines are
MLINE, MLSTYLE, and MLEDIT. Before executing the actual
MLINE command, you'll want to set up a multiline style. Similar to text or dimension styles, define the desired end result
before drawing the actual objects. Located in the Format pull-
down menu under Multiline Style... is the entrance to the

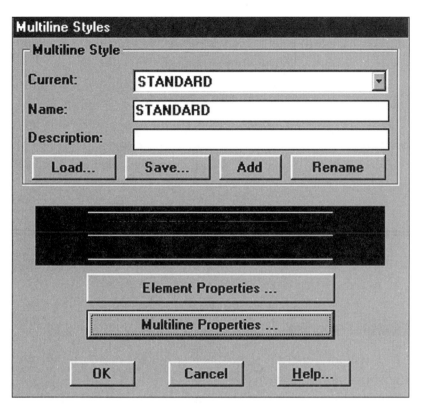

MLSTYLE command as shown in Figure 1. Die-hard keyboard-
ers can, of course, key in the command.

Consistent with other named styles, you'll recognize the
familiar "Standard" name. This style is fairly simple and made of
two elements one unit apart. Now, let's take a look at the
options available within it.

**Current:** Lists the name of the current multiline style. It is
also used to change the current style to any previously defined
style loaded in the drawing. If you've xref'd any drawings in
this drawing, some externally referenced multiline styles might
have come along with the drawing. Notice that the syntax is the
same as other externally referenced named objects.

**Name:** This area is used to enter the name of a new style you
want to add or save.

**Description:** Place a multiline style description in this
section of the dialog box (optional).

**Save:** To save a multiline style to a file for future use in another drawing, save it to an MLN file. *Acad.mln* is the default file name and is stored within the *Support* directory.

**Load:** This button is used to load a previously defined multiline style from an MLN file.

**Add:** This button adds a newly created style to the existing drawing. It also makes the designated style current.

**Rename:** You guessed it! Use this one to change the name of an existing style.

Notice a picture of the new style in the image tile. (Note: Linetypes, other than continuous, don't display in the image tile.)

Both Element Properties... and Multiline Properties... send you to a subdialog box.

## Element Properties

The Element Properties subdialog box sets the properties for the individual mline elements.

The Elements section of this dialog displays the properties and offset distance of each element. You'll notice the elements are always displayed in descending order (by offset distance). Now, Let's go through a review of the buttons.

**Add:** Adds a new element to the multiline style. By default, AutoCAD adds the elements at an offset of 0.

**Delete:** Removes the selected element from the style.

**Offset:** This Edit box lets you change the offset distance of the selected element. Double click in the box for quick replacement editing.

**Color:** When selected, this option will send you to the Select Color dialog box (DDCOLOR). The color selected will be assigned to the highlighted element. You can also key in the color name or number in the text box.

**Linetype:** Similar to Color, this option will display the Select Linetype dialog box (DDLTYPE). You can load and select a linetype within this dialog. The linetype selected will be assigned to the highlighted element. Notice that, unlike color, you can't key in the linetype name.

## Multiline Properties

This dialog is used to define properties of the entire multiline as a whole.

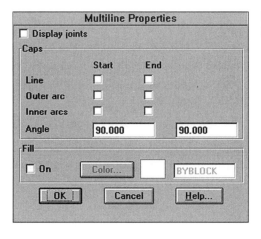

**Figure 2:** Element Properties dialog box.

If you would like AutoCAD to display a miter line at the corner joints, toggle the Display joints option on, as shown in Figure 2.

**Caps:** You can also choose to cap your multiline. Multilines can be capped from the beginning (startpoint) or at the end with either arcs or straight-line segments.

**Line:** Caps your multiline with a straight-line segment at the startpoint and/or endpoint.

**Outer arc:** Caps your multiline with an arc connecting the outermost elements.

**Inner arc:** If you have a multiline with at least four elements, AutoCAD will create an arc connecting between pairs of inner elements. If you have an uneven number of elements, the middle line will not be capped. For exam-ple, if you have six ele-ments in your multi-line, elements 2 and 5 will be connected with an inner arc. Elements 1 and 3 will also be connected, as shown in Figure 3.

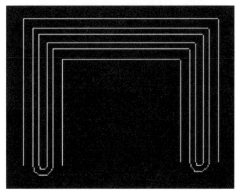

**Figure 3:** Capped Multiline.

**Angle:** This edit box controls the angle of the capping arc or line. Any value between 10 and 170 degrees is valid. I should warn you, changing the angle of capped arcs yields unusual results.

The Fill Panel permits you to turn on a background fill for your multilines, as well as control the Fill color. The Color... button sends you to the Select Color dialog box. (Note: Modifications made to the Fill panel do not display in the image tile in the Multiline Style dialog.)

After you've set your multiline to suit your needs, key in the name you desire for this style (over the existing one in the Name area), and add this style to the drawing. If you don't add it to the drawing, your changes will be disregarded. This new style will become current. (Note: If you want to save the multiline for use in other drawings, be sure to use the Save option.)

Now, you're ready to create your multilines. Under the Draw pull-down menu, you'll see multiline (or execute the MLINE command manually or from a toolbar). There are three options in the MLINE command: Justification, Scale, and Style. The default option is **<From point>:**—similar to the LINE command. Using the default, you can begin drawing your multilines on your drawing using the current multiline style. As you create multiline segments, you'll see this prompt: **Undo/<To point>:**, which allows you to undo multiline segments if you make an error.

There are three Justification options that determine how the multiline will be drawn between points: Top, Zero, and Bottom.

**Top:** Draws the multiline below the cursor. The element with the highest positive offset value is at the specified point.

**Zero:** Draws the multiline relative to the center line (the 0.0 origin point of the multiline).

**Bottom:** Draws the multiline above the cursor. The element with the smallest offset value is at the specified point.

You can also choose to Scale the overall width of the multiline. This scale factor multiplies the values set within the Multiline Style dialog box. For example, if you select a scale factor of

2 and your offsets are .25 and -.25, the end result would be an offset of .5 and -.5. The total width of the multiline doubles.

**Mline Trivia** (for you AutoCAD Jeopardy contestants!): A negative offset flips the order of the offset elements. This change puts the smallest offset on top (probably a negative offset). A negative scale value also alters the scale factor (by the absolute value). I think I'd prefer to create another style—it would require fewer brain cells. Here's one more for the trivia buffs: A scale factor of 0 will actually collapse the mline into a single line. I'm thinking LINE command, myself.

The Style option is used to switch from one existing multiline style to another. The style you specify must already be loaded or defined with the drawing.

Grips and multilines go well together. The Grips appear at the endpoints of the segments, based on the justification. You can use object snaps on multilines and the following standard editing commands: COPY, MOVE, MIRROR STRETCH, and EXPLODE. If you explode a multiline, it turns into ordinary line segments.

Because of the complexity of multilines, they have their own dialog box for editing. The MLEDIT command is located in the Modify pull-down menu under the object cascade.

The MLEDIT dialog box is made up of four columns—each with its own mission. The first column works on multilines that cross, the second on multilines that

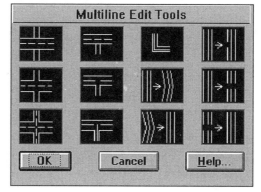

**Figure 4:** Multiline Edit.

form a T, The third on corner joints and vertices, and the fourth cuts or welds a multiline.

**Multilines that cross:** The three options are Closed Cross, Open Cross, and Merged Cross. The order in which you select

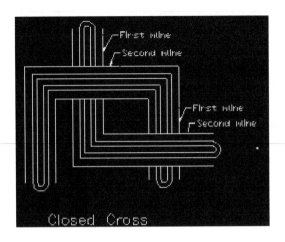

the crossing mlines
is very important.
The Golden mline
Editing Rule is: The
mline you want to
end up on top, is
selected last. The
order that they're
selected in is the
order in which
they'll be placed.
(The *User Reference
Manual* has this procedure documented incorrectly.)

Closed Cross is an excellent example. This option creates a
closed cross intersection between two multilines. You will be
prompted for a first and second mline. The second mline will
lay on top of the first one. This orientation will force Auto-
CAD to break the mline underneath and cement the two
together. If you find you've selected in the wrong order, take
advantage of the Undo option that is built inside of the
MLEDIT command.

With an Open Cross, the order of selection is still important.
An open cross breaks all the elements of the first multiline and
only the outside elements of the second multiline (see the
image tile in the dialog box).

The order of selection doesn't effect the results of a Merged
Cross. Both multilines are completely merged together.

**Multilines that form a T:** The second column of the
MLEDIT dialog box deals with Closed, Open, and Merged Ts.
The same Golden Rule listed for crosses applies to Ts (they are
pick dependent).

## Corner Joints

The Corner Joint option is used to create a nicely squared off
corner where two multilines meet. AutoCAD will trim (or

extend) the first multiline to its intersection with the second multiline. This is another example of being "pick dependent."

**Vertices:** Let's say you find you need to add an alcove to an existing room comprised of multilines. One quick fix would be using the Add Vertex option within MLEDIT. You could add four vertices and then use Grips to stretch the inner two vertices out to form a nice addition. New vertices don't display a change in the multiline, but using your grips, you'll see the new additions to the multiline. It's a simple matter of selecting the Add Vertex option within MLEDIT and picking on the multiline where you'd like the new vertex to go.

You can also delete an unwanted vertex. In MLEDIT, select the Delete Vertex option and AutoCAD will delete the vertex nearest to the selected point.

## Cutting and Welding

If you decide to insert a door within your mline, MLEDIT can be used to cut through one element at a time or all of them simultaneously. The Cut Single option prompts for two points to cut between. AutoCAD will only cut the element selected.

If you choose the Select All option, AutoCAD will cut through all the elements of the multiline. You will be prompted for two points as you were with Cut Single.

The opposite of Cutting is Welding. Should you make a mistake or change your mind after a Cut, you can always weld your mlines back together with the Weld All option. Simply pick the two points you want AutoCAD to weld between, and your mline will be as good as new!

If worse comes to worse and you're unable to get the proper results within the MLEDIT dialog box, you can always EXPLODE the mlines and use the standard editing commands. At that point, any command that works on lines will work on your multilines.

Mlines have been the victims of some bad press since Auto-CAD Release 13 came out. Though there's still room for improvement, mlines have much to offer in many different applications. Give mlines a try (I sound like an mline activist), and you might be surprised how they fit into your daily Auto-CAD routine.

# Crosshatching Revisited

The AutoCAD Release 12 BHATCH command revolutionized the way we crosshatched our drawings. There was no longer a need to spend countless hours creating and selecting boundaries in an effort to please the old **hatch** command. Suddenly, with the new BHATCH command (which was really an ADS routine that barely made it into Release 12), the boundaries were miraculously created for us.

AutoCAD Release 13 brought two new features to crosshatching: automatic island detection and associative hatching. This powerful new combination eliminated even more tedium.

AutoCAD Release 14 finally adds a solid filled pattern to it's extensive library list. In addition to that the overall crosshatching capabilities have been improved to produce more predictable results.

The Release 12 BHATCH melds the concept of ray casting with the world of hatching by giving users the necessary tools to select an internal point near the boundary of the enclosed area to crosshatch. To do this, AutoCAD sends out four rays in search of a boundary in the positive and negative *x*, *y* directions. The first ray to find an edge starts to formulate a polyline around the enclosed area. This procedure is called raycasting, and the newly created polyline is a **bpoly**. End users have been doing this same series of events manually for years, creating adhoc boundaries with the **pline** command, then using these boundaries to hatch. All other regions within the selected area also need to be individually selected to ensure proper results. We'll call these internal regions "islands" for future reference. After selecting the boundary and the islands the user would then apply the hatch pattern.

In the past, if you had to change the hatch pattern after it was applied, you were out of luck. The hatch pattern had to be erased and recreated with the modifications. If the boundaries were modified in any way, the crosshatching remained as it was originally created. The Release 12 crosshatching had no means for adapting to a changed boundary definition. Both of these issues were addressed in Release 13.

## The new BHATCH

Let's enter the BHATCH command from the Draw Pull-down menu. This will display the Boundary Hatch dialog box as shown in Figure 1. To view the various icons, pick on the hatch

**Figure 1:** The Boundary Hatch dialog box.

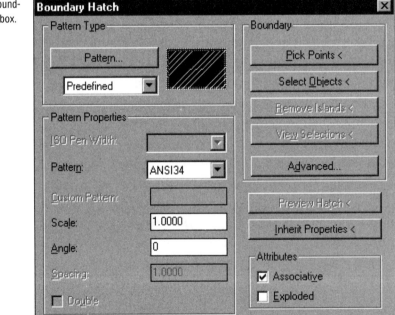

pattern image tile, which will step through them one at a time.
Or if you prefer, you can view the entire pallette of cross hatch
patterns by selecting the Pattern... option. You can also select
the pattern by name by picking the pattern pop-up listing. If
you go to the Pattern pallette, you'll see the new solid fill
option in the upper left-hand corner, as seen in Figure 2.
Should you select this new option, you may also notice that the
solid filled pattern displays the layer color from within the
BHATCH dialog (nice touch).

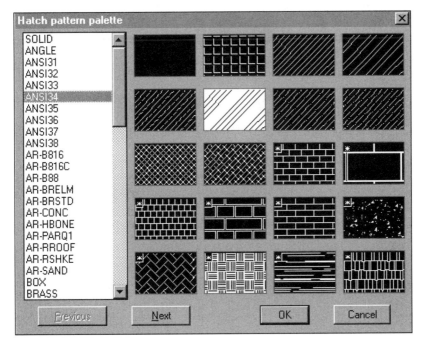

**Figure 2:** Hatch pattern palette dialog box.

As you leaf through the listing, note the ISO patterns that
were added to adapt for international standards requirements.
Selecting any of the ISO patterns also permits input in the ISO
Pen-width edit box. Adherence to ISO standards is another
Autodesk strategy for the globalization of AutoCAD.

Most of the options displayed on the left side of the dialog
box are self-explanatory and similar to the BHATCH command
of R13 and R12. Under "Pattern Type," you will find the User
defined and Predefined options along with a new Custom

option. Predefined utilizes the standard hatch patterns included in the ACAD.PAT file. User-defined lets you define a simple crosshatch pattern of lines on the fly. You determine the angle and spacing between the lines (Spacing and Angle edit boxes) and whether or not the crosshatch lines are to be double hatched (the Double option). Toggling on the double hatch option will draw a second set of lines perpendicular to the original defined lines.

Selecting the Custom pattern type will enable the Custom Pattern edit box. If you wish to use a custom hatch pattern (PAT file) that isn't part of the standard ACAD.PAT file, you may input this name. The rest of the process proceeds as usual.

If you want to insert any crosshatch patterns as individual line segments rather than block definitions, you may check the Explode option. It should be noted, however, that the associativity of the crosshatching will be lost by doing this, not to mention sending your entity count through the roof.

Jumping to the right side of the dialog you'll see the Inherit Properties button, which is the same as the Copy Existing Hatch button in Release 12, is used to duplicate the settings of an existing hatch pattern. This option is useful when editing another person's drawing where you aren't familiar with the hatch pattern settings. The Inherit Properties button will prompt you to select an existing hatch pattern and automatically fill in the dialog box with the proper information.

Notice the Associative toggle. You definitely want to select this option. Unselecting Associative will return you to the the primitive Release 12 world of hatching.

Select the Pick Points button (assuming you have a drawing to be crosshatched) and select an area you'd like to hatch. Notice how AutoCAD not only selects the boundary but the internal islands as well. This method is much easier than before. Should you prefer that AutoCAD ignore one or more islands, you can return to the dialog box and select the button that says Remove Islands, which will allow you to choose the internal regions you don't want crosshatched. The View Selections but-

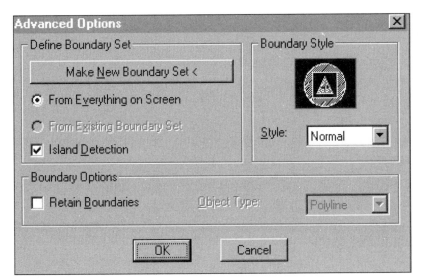

**Figure 3:** The BHATCH Advanced Options dialog box.

ton permits viewing of the currently defined boundaries. The "Advanced" button will send you to a subdialog box, as shown in Figure 3. This subdialog box allows you to return to the now primitive world of ray casting by turning island detection off. You can indicate whether you'd like the final boundary to be constructed with polylines or regions should you choose to retain the boundaries. You can define a specific boundary set if you feel the crosshatching procedure is too slow. Defining a boundary set will narrow the realm of entities that AutoCAD takes into consideration when searching for a boundary (speeding up the selection process).

The dialog box in Figure 3 contains your current style of hatching (Normal, Outermost, and Ignore). The default setting is Normal, which hatches every other group of boundaries from the outside in. Outermost crosshatches the outermost boundary only, and Ignore crosshatches through everything, regardless of any internal boundaries. The Advanced options dialog can also be used to toggle Retain Boundaries on or off. Warning: turning this feature on will greatly inhibit future boundary editing (leave it off!).

When the proper islands have been detected, select the preview button. If you need to modify the scale factor, angle or pattern, now is the time to do it. If all looks well, pick Apply to save it.

I must admit, however, that I miss the Another button in the Release 12 dialog box. This button permitted saving hatches without leaving the BHATCH command.

The BHATCH command adapts well to blocks and XREFs. There is no need to explode or bind the geometry because BHATCH will easily hatch any closed region. Occasionally a discrepancy occurs when the $x$ and $y$ scale factors of the block or XREF are not the same.

## On to Boundary

If you're used to using the **bpoly** command, you will need to get into the habit of using the **boundary** command. The boundary command acts identically to the **bpoly** command (in fact they both pull up the same dialog box). Although both commands are available in Release 13 and 14, I'd look for this command to be on the "termination" list for future releases.

You should try modifying the objects you've used as your boundary (move them and scale them) and see the crosshatch adapt to the change. Crosshatch patterns update even if they are on a layer that is frozen or off. There is, however, one rule to follow as you edit your boundaries. Don't open the boundary—it will result in a disassociation of your hatching.

As mentioned earlier, Release 12 didn't allow you to change your hatch pattern, scale, or angle after you applied it. You would need to erase the hatching and start the BHATCH process from the beginning. Release 13 and 14 offers the **hatchedit** command (Modify pull-down -Object cascade). Upon entering this command, you'll see a repeat of the original BHATCH dialog box with a few items grayed out. Make your changes and pick Apply—it's that simple.

You'll also find that Release 14 improved the editing capabilities to the extent that you can delete an island, and the crosshatching will reheal itself. Another nice R14 feature is the ability to turn off all of the hatching by setting FILLMODE to 0 (or OFF).

For programmers, AutoCAD has a command prompt interface that can be used when writing script files, menus, or Auto-LISP routines. Using a dash in front of the BHATCH command (or **boundary** and **hatchedit**) will execute a command prompt level interface rather than a dialog box.

**One final surprise:** the old **hatch** command is alive and well. In fact, it's been enhanced to accommodate point acquisition. If you want to quickly cross-hatch a section with no existing boundary, don't draw in a boundary to hatch, let the **hatch** command do it for you:

```
Command: hatch
Pattern (? or name/U,style) <ANSI31>:
Sale for pattern <1.000>:
Angle for pattern <0>:
Select hatch boundaries or <Return> for direct hatch
  option.
Select objects: enter
Retain polyline <N>:
From point:
Arc/Close/Length/Undo/<Next point>:
```

This new option will permit you to draw an adhoc area on the screen and crosshatch it. The area doesn't even need to be closed. If you choose to retain the polyline, you'll have a polyline around the edge of the hatch pattern. This hatching is not associative, however, and cannot be modified.

The crosshatching functionality in AutoCAD continues to get better and better.

# Text and Dtext

No matter what you do for a living, you can't get away from text. Some applications require laborious amounts of notes while others require just a few text strings here and there. Either way, you're faced with a decision. Which of the three text commands should you use? What are the pros and cons of each command? What about future edits? Should you do it the old way or should you try the new method?

This chapter will deal with the age-old text commands TEXT and DTEXT as well as the MTEXT command (Release 13 and 14). Hopefully, you'll gain some insight and learn some tricks you didn't know about. If you're a veteran user of AutoCAD, forget old habits and open your mind (you might find some time-saving tips).

The TEXT command has been in AutoCAD forever. Its interface is not too friendly—it's a command-prompt-driven command. No charming dialog box, no visual display on the drawing of the text you're inputting. When Dynamic TEXT was introduced to AutoCAD, few users resisted switching to the much friendlier DTEXT command. DTEXT was capable of displaying the text in the actual drawing area—using the correct font to boot. Paragraphs were easier to create. Even though DTEXT could be temporarily confusing when using the fit or aligned option, it was a great milestone from TEXT.

Then came MTEXT. A far cry from DTEXT, multiline text
provides the look and feel of a text editor built right into Auto-
CAD. The ability to control the color, font, and size of individual
words was something never permitted in AutoCAD before
Release 13. Top that off with a spell-checker, and you could
hardly ask for more (though, of course, we all do).

Let's step through the text progression, elaborating in more
detail on the TEXT and DTEXT commands. They both hold their
proper place in drawing annotation—let's make sure we know
where.

## DTEXT

DTEXT is still the most frequently used of the text commands
and the obvious choice for single lines of text (as opposed to
paragraphs). The text is stored in strings—editing the properties
of individual words is impossible. The user can select the style,
position, height, and angle of the text within the DTEXT
command. The options within the DTEXT command are:

```
Command: DTEXT
Justify/Style/<Start point>:
Height <0.2000>:
Rotation angle <0>:
Text: Sample
Text: Test
Text:
```

First, DTEXT will ask you to select a start point for the text.
By default, you are selecting a lower-left-hand corner justification for your text. Should you desire a different type of justification, you can get a listing by keying in **J**.

```
Justify/Style/<Start point>: J
Align/Fit/Center/Middle/Right/TL/TC/TR/ML/MC/MR/BL/BC/BR:
```

The justification options are overwhelming. There are 15 different options. You'll probably use three or four throughout
your CAD lifetime. Tables 1 and 2 show a basic explanation.

69

**Table 1.** Vertical Justification Abbreviations

| | |
|---|---|
| **L** | Denotes the start points of your text (justifying to the left). |
| **C** | Denotes the center line of your text. AutoCAD calculates the center by dividing the distance between the start and end points of your text in half. |
| **R** | Denotes the endpoint of your text (justifying to the right). |

**Table 2.** Horizontal Justification Abbreviations

| | |
|---|---|
| **T** | Denotes the top line of your text. AutoCAD assumes uppercase letters, even if your text string doesn't include any |
| **M** | Denotes the middle line of your text. Middle is calculated by dividing the distance from the top to the baseline (not bottom) in half. |
| **B** | Denotes the bottom line of your text string. Bottom is calculated using any descenders (text characters that fall below the baseline: y, j, q, p, g). |
| **baseline** | Denotes the baseline of your text string, excluding descenders. The five options that work via the baseline are the default (left justified), center, right, align, and fit. |

The Align and Fit options are quite different from the others. These two options are actually a little easier in the TEXT command. They tend to be deceiving when using DTEXT.

**Align.** Select the start and endpoints of your desired text string (relative to the baseline). You will not be prompted for text height or angle. After keying in the text string, AutoCAD will calculate the appropriate height to squeeze the text between the two end points. The fewer the characters, the larger the text height. The angle is also calculated by the angle between the two endpoints. Here are a few pitfalls of the Align option:

- You select the two endpoints in reverse order, and your text appears upside down.
- DTEXT doesn't calculate the final text height until you hit the final <Enter> and terminate the command. What you see on

the screen is definitely not what you get (so don't let it confuse you).

**Fit.** Similar to the Align option with one additional prompt: Height. You control the start and end point of the text and indicate the desired text. This option is great for title blocks where height should remain consistent but you're often squeezing text to fit into a small area. The Fit option could also modify the width factor of the characters. For example, if the start and end points of your text string are far apart, the text height is quite small, and you use only a few characters, you'll get short, squatty letters. Conversely, if you put the endpoints close together and give a very large height with many characters, the letters would be quite tall and thin. Once again, you don't really know what the final result is until you hit the final <Enter> and end the command.

**Justification Quiz.** What's the difference between Middle and MC (Middle Center)? MC calculates the insertion point horizontally from the baseline to the Top. Middle calculates the insertion point from the Bottom (where the descenders live) to the Top.

**Time Saving Tip.** When specifying a justification, it's not necessary to input the J option to specify the desired justification. You only enter J when you need to list the options. Here's an example:

```
Command: DTEXT
Justify/Style/<Start point>: TC
Top/center point:
```

**The Style Option.** You can change the current text style to another pre-existing text style (you can't create them in this option). You can also list any or all existing text styles by inputting a question mark:

```
Command: DTEXT
Justify/Style/<Start point>: S
Style name (or ?) <SIMPLEX>: ?
```

```
Text style(s) to list <*>:
Text styles:
Style name: SIMPLEX Font files: ROMANS.SHX
Height: 0.0000 Width factor: 1.0000 Obliquing angle: 0
Generation: Normal
Style name: STANDARD Font files: txt
Height: 0.0000 Width factor: 1.0000 Obliquing angle: 0
Generation: Normal
Current text style: SIMPLEX
```

A Generation of Normal indicates that the style is not upside-down or backwards.

**Height.** After specifying the justification and insertion point, you'll be prompted for text height (unless you picked the Align option). The height can be shown by selecting a point on the screen, or it can be input manually.

**Rotation Angle.** The Rotation angle can also be selected on the screen or input manually. The rotation angle is calculated relative to the current angle 0. If you've moved angle 0 (perhaps to North) in the UNITS command, the text will be measured relative to this new setting. The Rotation angle option doesn't appear if you justified using Align or Fit.

**Text.** By the time you get to the Text: option, a vertical bar should appear on your screen. This bar is the size you indicated as the text height. As you key in characters for your text string, the bar will move across the screen. If you backspace, the characters disappear one step at a time. Pressing <Enter> takes you down to the next line (for paragraphs of text). You can move the text bar anywhere on the screen by moving the crosshairs to another location and picking on your screen. This setup permits placement of multiple lines of text all over your drawing without needing to re-enter the DTEXT command. When you've input all the desired text, hitting <Enter> twice will complete the command. The first <Enter> takes you down to the next line, and the second returns you to the command prompt.

DTEXT always displays left-justified until you hit the final <Enter>. After the final <Enter>, the text will be as you designed.

This option can be confusing to the unsuspecting user, but be patient and eventually the text will position itself correctly. Keep in mind that the text on the screen is temporary and isn't stored within your drawing until you hit the final <Enter>. Should you issue a Cancel to exit the command, all of the text will disappear. You must exit the DTEXT command using <Enter> to keep the input text.

For those of you using Release 12 or Release 13 for Windows, you can drag and drop text from a text editor using these simple steps:

- Create and save your text file.
- Enter the DTEXT command and answer all the prompts until the Text: option.
- Drag and Drop the text file (you can use File Manager to grab the file) into AutoCAD.

The text will appear on the screen using the current Text style. If you drag and drop without entering the DTEXT command in Release 13 or 14, AutoCAD will bring the text in as an MTEXT entity. Release 12 permits the use of the clipboard with the DTEXT command, which is done via an option in the Edit pull-down menu called Paste Command. To use this method, follow these steps:

- Highlight the desired text in your text editor.
- Copy to the clipboard (<Ctrl+C>).
- Enter the DTEXT command, and answer all the prompts until the Text: option.
- Select the Paste Command option from the Edit menu.
- The text will appear on the screen using the current Text style.

This method allows you to bring in partial files. Neither Release 12 nor 13 supports <Ctrl+V> to paste using DTEXT. The MTEXT command provides complete Clipboard compliance. The TEXT command doesn't support drag and drop or using the Clipboard.

## TEXT

By far the most primitive, the TEXT command is still invaluable when programming AutoCAD. I'd venture to say that a good portion of your customized menus and LISP routines are using TEXT behind the scenes to do their magic. Unbeknownst to many, you can create paragraphs with TEXT (a good tip for LISP routines). The command looks identical to DTEXT, but we'll step through it to show how to do paragraphs:

```
Command: TEXT
Justify/Style/<Start point>:
Height <2.6602>:
Rotation angle <0>:
Text: Plain old
Command:TEXT
Justify/Style/<Start point>: enter
Text: AutoCAD text
```

To force text below the previously drawn text string, hit an extra <Enter> at the Start point. This method can also be used in DTEXT, in case you accidentally leave the command and want to pick up where you left off.

**Control Codes.** Both TEXT and DTEXT use special control codes to input those oft-needed characters not found on the keyboard. Control codes can also be used to underline or overscore your text strings. There are six predefined control codes available. All control codes begin with %% to inform AutoCAD you're issuing a special code. It doesn't matter whether the following character is upper or lower case.

%% o   Toggles overscore on/off.

%% u   Toggles underscore on/off.

%% d   Draws degree symbol (°).

%% c   Draws a center/diameter symbol (Ø).

%% p   Draws the plus/minus tolerance symbol (±).

%% %   Forces a single percent sign (believe it or not).

Autodesk chose two percent signs as a control code indicator believing it was highly unlikely that anyone would need that unusual combination. If you insist on using two percent signs in your text strings, you can use three percent signs to force one (%%%=%). A total of six percent signs would be needed to get two (%%%%%% =%%).

To indicate to AutoCAD that you want to write the text string 98° while in the TEXT or DTEXT command, you would type:

```
Text: 98%%d
```

5±±.001 would be written as

```
Text: 5%%P.001
```

Underscoring and overscoring are slightly different because they are toggles. The first instance of the control code toggles the under/overscoring on, and the second instance toggles it off. If there is no second instance, the entire line of text is underscored (not the entire paragraph). AutoCAD would be created using the following code:

```
Text: %%UAutoCAD
```

If you want to underline just part of a line, as in "AutoCAD is a great tool," you would use the following code:

```
Text: %%uAutoCAD%%u is a great tool.
```

When using DTEXT, the control codes don't display in their final state until you complete the command (so don't panic when all these percent signs show up on your screen).

# The Magical
# World of MTEXT

All applications annotate their drawings in some way.
We've already explored the TEXT and DTEXT commands, their pros and cons, and their place in the text
world. TEXT and DTEXT are available in AutoCAD Releases 9
through 14 and are still the favorites of veteran AutoCAD users.
Multiline Text provides many annotation advantages we've
never had before.

Each line of text in the TEXT and DTEXT commands is considered one object, in the form of a text string. Though DTEXT
permits paragraph creation, each line is still an individual
object. Not so with MTEXT. Multiline text is exactly that—text
with many lines. All the lines together comprise one object. All
the lines move together, copy together, and so on. However,
due to the advanced nature of MTEXT, we can edit individual
lines, words, and even individual characters. MTEXT permits
changing such properties as color, font, or height down to the
character level. Text entities of the past have never had such
capabilities.

Unfortunately, MTEXT was somewhat buggy in the early
stages of Release 13. This instability caused many users to shy
away from the new command. Fear no more, MTEXT is stable
and should be a command you use often. Since we've been
using DTEXT for years, it's difficult to make this transition to

the better MTEXT world. It will take time and practice before you feel as comfortable using MTEXT as you have with DTEXT.

MTEXT can be accessed by typing in T at the command prompt or by selecting DRAW=>TEXT=> Multiline text from the menu. You can also access MTEXT from the DRAW toolbar, selecting the button in the lower right-hand corner marked with an A. Though the pull-down and toolbar buttons read TEXT, they're executing the MTEXT command. Autodesk is really pushing MTEXT to be the standard for drawing annotation. The Dimension text objects are all MTEXT objects.

MTEXT starts with a command-line interface, then launches into a dialog box (it is one of the only commands to do so). Let's review the command-line options first:

```
Command: mtext
Current text style: STANDARD. Text height: 0.2000
Specify first corner:
Specify opposite corner or
   [Height/Justify/Rotation/Style/Width]:
```

MTEXT uses a bounding box to determine the placement of text. You define a rectangle, and AutoCAD uses this rectangle to determine insertion point and line width. Text is permitted to spill out of the rectangle. The direction of the spill is controlled by the justification (or attachment) and indicated with an arrow. Let's tour each of these options.

**Height:** This option is used to specify a new text height, which can also be changed within the MTEXT dialog box.

**Justify:** Justify is used to select the justification options (equate this to the Justification option in DTEXT). MTEXT uses Top Left justification by default. Not all of the DTEXT justification options exist in MTEXT. All of the options aren't necessary because MTEXT uses a bounding box to define text placement. Should you select the Justification option, you'll receive an additional prompt of justification options.

**TL/TC/TR/ML/MC/MR/BL/BC/BR:** These abbreviations are the same as those in the DTEXT or TEXT commands:

| T | Top |
|---|---|
| **M** | Middle |
| **B** | Bottom |
| **L** | Left |
| **C** | Center |
| **R** | Right |

**Figure 1:** Command abbreviations as they relate to the MTEXT bounding box.

Figure 1 shows the abbreviations as they relate to the MTEXT bounding box. All Top justification options spill downwards out of the bounding box. Middle justification options spill up and down evenly. Bottom justification options spill upwards out of the bounding box. For example, TL stands for Top

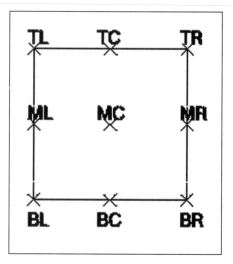

Left. The text is justified from the upper-left corner and extra text will spill downwards. MR stands for Middle Right. The text is justified by the middle right side of the bounding box. Text spills up and down. After selecting an attachment option, the MTEXT command returns to the original options, allowing other modifications.

**Rotation:** Select this option if you want to change the rotation angle for the text. Unlike TEXT or DTEXT, the MTEXT command always resets the rotation angle back to zero after the command is executed.

**Style:** Use this option to change to another existing text style. It does not let you create a new style.

**Width option:** Specify the MTEXT object width by keying in the numeric answer or picking on the screen.

**Other corner:** Pick the opposite corner of the rectangular bounding box. It doesn't matter whether you pull the box up or

**Figure 2:** The Edit MTEXT dialog box contains many options we never had in DTEXT.

down, you're only specifying the width at this time. Remember, MTEXT will spill outside of the bounding box.

The Edit MTEXT dialog box contains many options we never had in DTEXT as seen in Figure 2. We can change the fonts, color, height, and much more of individual sentences, words, or characters. Many of the buttons send you to other dialog boxes. You'll notice that the MTEXT dialog box is made up of three tabs:  Character, Properties, and Find/Replace

The MTEXT dialog box works the same way your favorite text editor does. If you've selected a truetype font, you'll be able to Bold, Italicize, and underline by highlighting the desired text and selecting the appropriate button.

You'll notice the Undo button that lets you undo your previous operation followed by the stack/unstack button. The ability to stack characters (much like a fraction) was introduced in Release 13. While it is confusing at first, it's actually easy to do when you understand how it works. Stacking is controlled by the forward slash or the Carat symbol (^). Using the forward slash stacks the characters and separates them with a bar. The Carat symbol stacks them without a bar, as shown in Figure 3. Key in the desired stacking text, highlight, and pick the Stack button.

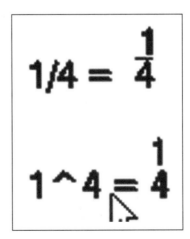

**Figure 3:** Examples of stacked fractions.

79

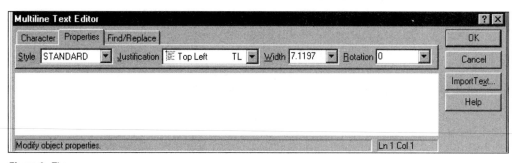

**Figure 4:** The settings in the Properties tab control the default values for all the text.

You'll notice the color option (which defaults to bylayer) followed by the Symbol pull-down menu. The Symbol pull-down makes it easy to insert your favorite character. Selecting Other... will send you to the Windows character map where you pick from a wide selection of characters (especially in wing-dings)

The Import text button is used to bring in an external text file. This option will send you to the Import File dialog box so you can select the file to bring into MTEXT. (Text can also be copied to the clipboard and pasted into MTEXT using <Ctrl+C> and <Ctrl+V>.)  Release 14 supports Rich Text Format (.RTF) files.

**Properties tab:** This tab contains the overall property settings for your text. These are the same options available to you when you first entered the MTEXT command.

**Find/Replace tab:** You'll find this section acts much the same as your word processor.  You select the word(s) to find and the word(s) to replace and AutoCAD does the rest for you. You can specify whether or not you want AutoCAD to follow case sensitivity or search for whole words.

Heads-up—if you cancel out of the MTEXT dialog box, all text will be lost.

All of the text created within one MTEXT command is one object to AutoCAD. When editing the text, you will do so by editing the entire object. The DDEDIT command is probably the quickest method for modifying an MTEXT object as it quickly pulls up the MTEXT dialog box for editing. The Modify pull-down has an Object=>Text option you can use to execute the

DDEDIT command. You can also use DDMODIFY or the Properties toolbar button to edit MTEXT. These commands permit editing of all the features in the original MTEXT dialog box.

MTEXT and Grips work very well together. If you've ever needed to change the width of a paragraph in DTEXT, you know how difficult it is. It's easier to erase the text and start all over. With MTEXT, it's simple. Select the MTEXT object at the command prompt to activate grips. Make one of the outer grips hot by selecting it. Notice how you can stretch the rectangle? Try changing the size of the rectangle and notice how the text rewraps to accommodate the new size.

For those of you who indulge in customizing, MTEXT can also be accessed completely via the command line interface (no dialog box) by executing the command with a dash in front of it. For example:

```
Command: -MTEXT
```

MTEXT is a valuable tool;  it's almost like having a word processor built right into AutoCAD. Be sure to leave DTEXT aside periodically and familiarize yourself with the new MTEXT dialog box. It takes minimal practice to feel comfortable working in this new environment. Expect to see even more functionality in MTEXT in the future.

# Text Tips
# and Tricks

What's the difference between a style and a font? Can you temporarily change your slow TrueType fonts to a faster font while in production mode? What do all those text variables actually do. In this chapter we'll take our base knowledge even further by discussing the many other aspects surrounding text.

## Text Fonts Versus Styles

A text font defines the shape of the text characters. AutoCAD supports TrueType fonts, Adobe Type 1 PostScript fonts, and its own SHX fonts. Previous releases of AutoCAD do not support TrueType fonts. The early releases of AutoCAD read only those text fonts based on shape files, which have no fill capabilities. PostScript fonts were a great addition to AutoCAD in theory, but in practice, they often had inconsistent text heights. The new TrueType font support permits not only use of the TTF fonts that come with AutoCAD but of other TrueType fonts (including the Windows Wingdings font).

The TEXT and DTEXT commands do not allow you to use font files directly—you must create a style with them first. The MTEXT command uses the current text style as you initially input the text but permits overriding selected characters with a different font. A text style sets up many parameters for your text, such as an obliquing angle, fixed text height, and of course, the text font of your choice. You might have many text styles that use the same text font. One style might have an obliquing angle (or slant) of 30 degrees, another style might have an obliquing angle of 45, but both use the same font.

The Text Style dialog box command can be found in the Format pull-down menu. Let's take a look at the new Text Style dialog box as seen in Figure 1:

**Style Name:** Text style names can be up to 31 characters in length (though I'd keep them short and sweet). They may contain letters, numbers, and some special characters, such as dollar sign ($), underscore (_), hyphen(-), and so on. The name of text fonts, on the other hand, must be the name of existing text fonts AutoCAD can find through the usual search process. To create a new style select the New option and key in the desired name. By default AutoCAD will use the name of Style1, Style2, etc.

**Font name:** To set a type style, you select from the drop down list in the Text Style dialog box. This dialog box will search for SHX, PFA, PFB, and TTF files (AutoCAD fonts, Post-Script, and TrueType).

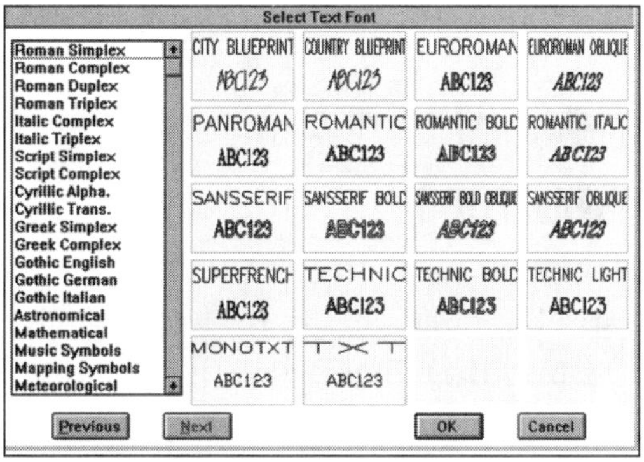

**Figure 1:** The Release 12 icon menu.

After selecting a font, the character preview set will update. The TrueType fonts also have the added feature of applying a font style such as bold or italic to the selected font.

## Character Preview

AutoCAD assumes a character preview set of "AaBbCc. . ." To view a particular word or set of characters, you can key in a replacement set over the existing set in the text box. Select the Preview button to view the new set of characters.

**Effects:** The Effects section of the dialog box contain additional control over your text. Let's review the various options.

**Height <0.0000>:** You may choose to set a fixed or variable text height. When a style with a fixed text height is used, the MTEXT, TEXT, and DTEXT commands will no longer prompt you for text height. If you want to use a variety of text heights with the same text style, leave the height at zero. It is a frequent mistake of new users to immediately place a fixed text value in the STYLE command. This mistake is followed by frustration when the DTEXT command no longer permits changing the text height. Set a fixed text height only when you want to assign a specific text height to a style.

**Width factor <1.0000>:** A width factor greater than 1 will stretch the characters, a value less than 1 will compress the characters, as shown in Figure 3. You might find it useful to set the width factor to a value less than 1 when you need to place many characters in a small area but do not desire to change the height.

**Figure 3:** A width factor greater than 1 will stretch the characters, and a value less than 1 will compress the characters.

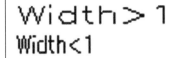

**Obliquing angle <0>:** The obliquing angle option in the STYLE command controls the slant of the characters. A positive obliquing angle will slant the text forward (to the right), and a negative obliquing angle will slant the text backwards (to the left), as shown in Figure 4.

**Figure 4:** A positive obliquing angle will slant the text forward (to the right), and a negative obliquing angle will slant the text backwards (to the left).

The angle is actually an offset from 90 degrees and must be in the range of -85 degrees to +85 degrees. This ability is very useful when drawing isometrics, where it's very important that the text lie on a particular isometric plane.

**Backwards? <N>:** The STYLE command also allows you to

force your text to be written backwards (right to left). This setup would create mirrored text, occasionally used in PC design and moldings.

**Upsidedown? <N>:** Fairly straightforward, this option is used to force text creation to be upside down.

**Vertical? <N>:** By default, AutoCAD creates horizontal orientation text. Text can also be placed vertically, one character below the other. Each successive line of text is placed to the right of the preceding line, rather than below the preceding line. When in the various text commands, you'll notice that the default text rotation angle is set to 270 degrees when using a vertical text style, as shown in Figure 5. Not all text fonts support vertical orientation.

The Delete option is an easy way to get rid of unwanted Text styles. Heretobefore this could only be done through the Purge command.

The Apply button will apply all changes to the current selected style. If you forget to apply and select the Close button to exit, AutoCAD will remind you that you haven't saved the changes and will ask you if you want to apply the changes to the current style.

If you change the font or vertical property of an existing text style, all existing text using that style will be updated. Changing the style properties, such as height and obliquing angle, will not affect existing line text (DTEXT or TEXT objects)—only that of subsequent text. MTEXT, on the other hand, will apply changes to width and obliquing angle to existing text.

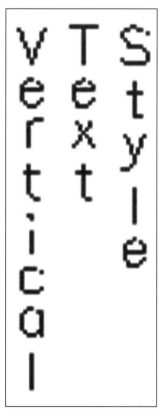

**Figure 5:** The default text rotation angle is set to 270 degrees when using a vertical text style.

85

**Figure 6:** The Text
Style dialog box.

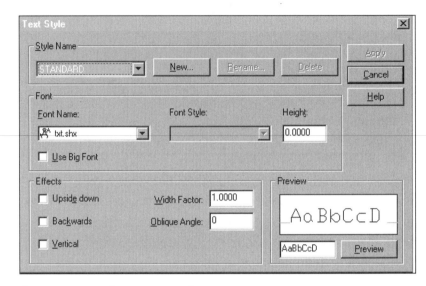

**Figure 6:** The Text Style dialog box.

## Changing the Current Text Style (Release 12 and 13)

The current text style can also be changed from within the TEXT, DTEXT, or MTEXT commands via the Style option. For example:

```
Command: DTEXT
Justify/Style/<Start point>: S
Style name (or ?) <TITLE>: TEST
Justify/Style/<Start point>:
```

And, of course, you can use the STYLE command to set a new current style, because it sets whichever style you create to be current.

Text styles can be renamed within the DDRENAME or RENAME commands.

## Miscellaneous Text System Variables

Release 13 added a few text system variables that relate to text, and fonts in particular.

**Textqlty** controls the resolution of TrueType and PostScript fonts. The accepted value range is between 0 and 100 with a default value of 50. A setting of 100 sets the resolution to 600 dpi, 50 to 300 dpi, and so on. The higher the setting, the finer the resolution, and the slower the regeneration. As you lower the value of textqlty, you'll notice the text will appear more jagged (but you'll regenerate faster). If you feel your TrueType fonts are really slowing you down, tampering with textqlty might help you out.

**Textfill** is used to fill (or not fill) the TrueType and PostScript fonts. When textfill is set to 0 (default), the text appears in outline form. When textfill is set to 1, the text is filled in (after the next regeneration). Filled-in TrueType fonts look great but can really slow you down.

**Qtext** (Quick Text) can be found in the Preferences dialog box on the Performance tab. When qtext is set to 1 (or on), the existing text will change to bounding rectangles on the next regeneration. In drawings with a great deal of text, this option could improve your speed dramatically. The rectangles let you view the placement of text without slowing you down.

You might notice that the discussion of these mistakes revolves around regeneration speeds and fonts. A decrease in speed accompanies the addition of TrueType fonts. The fontmap system variable can be used to temporarily map the slower fonts to a simpler, faster font. Then, when you're ready to plot, you can easily map the text back to its original font. You will need to create a font-mapping file first. This file can easily be created in a text editor (Notepad or EDIT will work). AutoCAD expects a file with an extension of *.map*, though it will read whatever file you indicate. (AutoCAD documentation incorrectly states that font mapping files have an extension of .fmp.)

The actual file contents are simple: The existing font is entered first (the slower font) followed by the destination font. The two are separated with a semicolon. Here's an example of a simple map file called example.map:

```
swissi.ttf; romans
system.ttf;txt
```

This file would map the swiss.ttf font of your current drawing to the simpler romans and the *system.ttf* font to txt. The name of the mapping file needs to be saved to the fontmap system variable. You can also input the name in the Preferences dialog box (Windows) under the Files tab.

When you want to return to the original fonts, simply delete the mapping choice from the Preferences dialog box or return the fontmap system variable to ".".

The fontalt system variable was a nice addition to Release 13. Fontalt is used to set a default alternative font. Have you ever opened a drawing to find that you were missing one of the fonts included in it? You had to instruct AutoCAD which font you would use as a replacement for the missing font. The fontalt system variable can be used to set a default font for just such instances so you aren't faced with the inconvenience.

Let's look at one more obscure system variable: fflimit controls the maximum number of TrueType or PostScript fonts AutoCAD stores in memory at any one time. It does not, however, control the maximum number of fonts you can use in a drawing. The default setting of 0 sets the value to unlimited. If you set it to 5, only five fonts would be stored for quick access. Additional fonts could force AutoCAD to page out to disk, thus slowing down performance.

On the other hand, it could free up memory for other uses. If you're not using your fonts for awhile, by all means, free up some memory by setting fflimit to a low value!

Very few applications squeak by without using some type of text within their drawings. Hopefully these minor text adjustments and explanations will help make life annotating your drawings just a little bit easier.

# Making You a Little More Dangerous

# Object Grips

Grips are one of the most powerful editing tools available in AutoCAD (and AutoCAD LT) to date. You might not agree, instead seeing grips as those annoying blue boxes that appear when you least expect them. If so, chances are you may not fully understand them. However, with a little patience, an open mind, and a little help from this chapter, I hope you'll see the light and be on your way to faster, more efficient editing habits.

Grips permit fast and effective editing in the following areas: Move, Copy, Rotate, Stretch, Scale, and Mirror. Grips eliminate the tedious steps you're used to while throwing in some automatic object snaps as well. Let's give them a try.

Be sure your grips are on by using the grips dialog box (in the Tools pull-down menu) and selecting the Enable Grips box as seen in Figure 1. You may also key in the command GRIPS and set it to 1. If you think you have modified the grip colors or size, use the grips dialog box to change Unselected... grips to blue and Selected... grips to red. Blue is a good color for grips because it doesn't distract from the drawing objects selected.The size of the grip boxes should be large enough to see easily but not so large they overwhelm (about one third across the slider bar should do).

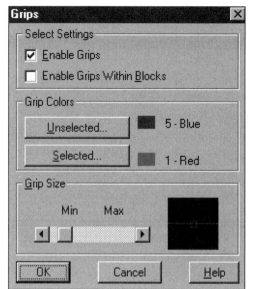

**Figure 1:** Object Grips dialog box.

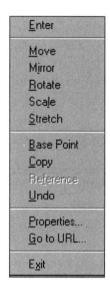

**Figure 2:** Object Grips right-click menu.

## Starting simple

We'll draw three objects: a line, arc, and circle. Grips live at the command prompt. They cannot be used while in an existing standard AutoCAD command. As soon as you enter a standard AutoCAD command (except for REDRAW), all your grips will disappear from the screen. While at the command prompt, pick the line with your input device. Three blue boxes will show up on your line, one at each endpoint and one at the midpoint.

There are three different types of grips: hot, warm, and cold. When grips are warm, they're ready to be edited. Notice as you move your cursor within the range of any grip how you're pulled in as though a magnet resided at each grip point. Pick one of the endpoint grips, and you'll see the grip has turned red. You guessed it—this is a hot grip. Selecting a hot grip enters the grip mode, and you're ready to pick the editing mode you desire.

Reviewing the graphics screen, you'll notice at the top of the screen, on the status line, the word "Stretch". You'll also see

91

that the word "stretch" is down in the command-prompt area. If you're using Release 12 DOS, notice the screen menu has changed to reflect the Grip editing options. If you are using Windows, you might consider turning your screen menu on in the Preferences dialog box (if you haven't already done so). Notice as you pull your cursor around that you're stretching the line (turn Ortho off for greater flexibility). Hit the space bar and you'll see that "stretch" has been replaced with "move" in both locations. As you move your cursor you're in Move mode, hit the space bar again, and you're in Rotate mode. Continue hitting the space bar to try Scale, Mirror, and return to Stretch. Grip mode will loop until you select an option. While in stretch mode, pick on your screen where you'd like the new endpoint to go. After picking, you're back at the command prompt and back to warm grips.

To make your grips go away, hit the escape key two times. Do one escape at a time and see how the grips remain blue but the object is no longer highlighted. Now the grips are cold. This object is not ready for editing. One more escape and all your grips will disappear.

The grip options display in the following order:
- Stretch
- Move
- Rotate
- Scale
- Mirror

If you know you want to mirror and don't want to page through each option to get there, you can proceed directly to Mirror keying in MI. Keying in the first two characters of any option will take you to your desired mode. Don't try this unless you have already selected a hot grip. If you're using AutoCAD Release 14, you may use the great new right click menu to select the mode of your choice as seen in Figure 2.

Now, pick the arc on your display. While at the command prompt, pick the edge of the arc to display the three grips. Make

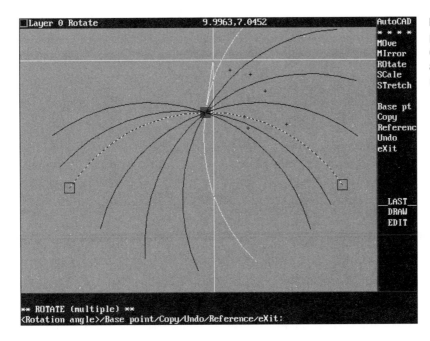

**Figure 3:** In this photo, the arc was copied by selecting C at the prompt and rotating the arc.

a hot grip out of the midpoint grip by picking it. Space through the options to see the different results of each editing selection. Return to the Rotate option. Notice in the command prompt area that there are several options available within the Rotate option:

    <Rotation angle>/Base point/
     Copy/Undo/Reference/eXit: C

All editing options have additional selection parameters available. Key in C for Copy (or pick Copy from the screen menu on the right). Now, as you pick while rotating the arc, you'll get multiple copies of the arc, as shown in Figure 3. This method is similar to using the Polar option in the ARRAY command. When you've made several copies, hit <Enter> to return to the command prompt (or X to exit). Only the original arc has warm grips. Hitting the escape key twice makes the grips disappear.

At the command prompt, pick the circle and notice the five grips that appear: one at each quadrant and one at the middle. Make a hot grip in the middle and page through each option finishing at the Scale option. Scale the circle down by a scale factor of .5.

What if I wanted to move the left grip of the circle to the right endpoint of the line? If I want to edit (move) the circle and use the grips on the line to do so, I'll need both warm and cold grips. The line will need to have cold grips (I don't want to move the line), and the circle will need warm grips.

Pick the line and the circle so they both have grips. To make the grips on the line cold, you'll hold down the shift key and pick the line (but not on a grip). This selection will turn the line cold. Now the circle remains as the only object that will actually be edited.

Make the grip at nine o'clock on the circle hot by picking it. Hit the space bar to change to the Move option. Move your cursor until the circle locks into place at the end of the line. The quadrant at nine o'clock on the selected circle falls at exactly the endpoint of the line. All this done with no object snaps!

Make all the grips disappear and reselect the circle. Make a hot grip on one of the quadrants. While in Stretch mode, hold down the shift key while picking a point on the screen. The shift key assumes the Multiple mode (like picking C for copy) and emulates the OFFSET command. The shift key used with any of the grip editing commands places you in Multiple mode.

Grips appear at different points on different objects. Because a polyline is one continuous object, the grips appear at each vertex. Stretching the individual vertices of a polyline is much easier with grips than using any of the standard AutoCAD commands. Notice how the grips appear on the original frame of a spline curve rather than the curve itself. There's no faster method of manipulating a spline curve than with grips. Grips leave the PEDIT command in the dust!

Draw a vertical dimension (associative dimensioning must be on). Notice that grips don't function at the dim prompt. Returning to the command prompt, select the dimension to display its grips. The grip selected as the hot grip will make all the difference in the world with dimension objects. If you select one of the dimension-line grips, you'll only be moving the dimension line location. Picking an extension-line grip permits relocating the selected extension line, which would modify the dimension value as well. If you want to move the dimension text, pick the grip on the text and move it to the desired location. Editing dimensions with grips is very flexible and efficient.

Returning to the grips dialog box, pick the checkbox labeled Enable grips within Blocks. Insert a Block, and display its grips. Many grips will display, and any of these may be used as your hot grip. Don't be fooled into thinking that you can edit the individual objects of the Block without exploding it. Grips don't permit breaking any standard AutoCAD rules. I would suggest returning to the grips dialog box and turning this feature off— all those grips get very confusing.

Sometimes the hot grip is not the desired base point for the object we're editing. All the grip editing modes provide the additional option of base point as a selection. For example, if I want to mirror a library symbol, Grip mode assumes I want to mirror around the hot grip. The axis I want to mirror around is

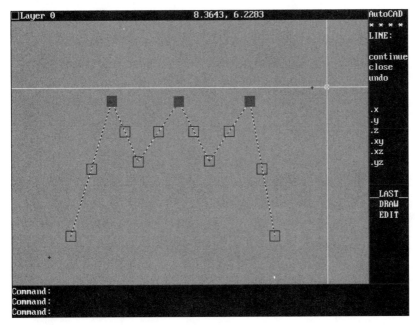

**Figure 4:** Holding the shift key down when selecting grips affords you the flexibility of choosing more than one.

not near the hot grip. I can use the base point option to change the first point of the mirror axis to suit my needs.

Grips permit stretching off of one hot grip at a time. Sometimes you may need to stretch at two or more different locations within the same stretch procedure, which would require more than one hot grip. Holding the shift key down while selecting existing grips will enable you to select more than one hot grip, as shown in Figure 4.

## One More Grip Tip

Grips are smart enough to remember and repeat preselected angles, distances, and scale factors. Returning to the line you've already drawn, display the grips. Make the midpoint grip hot and go to Rotate. Pick the Copy option (notice the command prompt indicates with **COPY (multiple)**. We are going to explicitly key in 20 for a 20-degree rotation angle. Our magical shift key will come into play one more time. Holding down the shift key and moving the cursor around the two lines, you'll notice an auxiliary snap occurring at 20-degree increments. Pick while holding down the shift key, and you'll find yourself making evenly spaced copies of the line as you move around in a circular fashion.

The shift key also remembers distances while copying or mirroring. Say I want to make five copies of a desk Block, each eight feet apart. I would pick the desk, make a hot grip, and use the Move, Copy option to input the first distance of @8'<90 (eight feet up at an angle of 90 degrees). After the original distance is set, I can use the shift key to copy the remaining desks into place—all at eight-foot increments.

The shift key is important and provides four functions:
- Place you into Multiple mode, while editing (same as COPY).
- Repeat the last distance or angle while editing.
- Permit the selection of more than one hot grip for stretching.
- Turn warm objects cold.

All grip editing functions provide an Undo option to undo the effects of the last step. An Undo at the command prompt undoes the editing that took place in the last grip mode—so be careful. Realize also that you didn't execute a standard Auto-CAD command at the prompt to get into grips. Don't make the mistake of hitting <Enter> at the command prompt to get back into grip mode. It will repeat the last standard AutoCAD command instead of entering grip mode and, most likely, all your grips will disappear. The only way to enter grip editing mode is to select a hot grip.

If you're dealing with a standard AutoCAD setup, the Pickfirst variable will be on. If you also have objects with grips highlighted when you go into the ERASE command, AutoCAD will assume the grip objects are those you want to erase. Soon those valuable objects will vanish. Always turn the grips cold (escape key) before entering a standard editing command.

Experiment with grips—force yourself to use them. Even if you're not willing to invest the time to becoming a grip expert, there's no effort required to quickly move Blocks or text objects around on your drawings using the simplest of grip fundamentals. AutoCAD provides many roads to the same end—some faster than others. Using grips is just another road along the route of efficient editing.

# Creating Curves (without NURBS)

Creating curves in AutoCAD is an integral part of many applications. The splines of the past were acceptable, though sometimes difficult to control and edit without proper understanding. This chapeter will review linear Splines, Fit Curves and the ellipses of Release 12. AutoCAD Release 13 used NURBS technology to renovate our splines and ellipses.

Splines in Release 12 (and before) begin their lives as polylines. We create an estimated frame using the PLINE command, and use the PEDIT command to turn it into a spline curve. Though our completed spline resembles a smooth curve, in reality it doesn't contain a single arc. The finished Release 12 spline consists of multiple straight polyline segments creating an approximated curve. Let's create a simple polyline spline and delve into its properties and characteristics. Create a simple control frame with a polyline, as shown in Figure 1. This frame consists of 8 control points (vertices).

The PEDIT (polyline edit) command is used to turn our frame into a spline. Select the frame and use the Spline option to get the result in Figure 2:

```
Command: PEDIT
Select polyline:
Close/Join/Width/Edit vertex/Fit/Spline/ Decurve/Ltype
   gen/Undo/eXit <X>: S
```

The Decurve option would return the spline to its original state.

The control frame still exists, but by default it is not displayed. It's easier to understand the inner-workings of a polyline spline (hereafter called a polyspline) if we turn the control frame back on. The system variable **splframe** controls the visibility of spline frames (for all types of splines). Set **splframe** to 1:

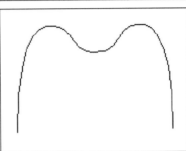

**Figure 1:** A simple control frame.

**Figure 2:** Using the PEDIT command to turn the control frame into a spline.

```
Command: SPLFRAME
New value for SPLFRAME<0>: 1
Command: REGEN
```

After regenerating and zooming in on the display, you'll see the control frame has returned. Let's discuss the resulting spline curve. Notice the spline starts and ends in the same location as the first and last vertex of the control frame. Imagine a magnet at each of the vertices pulling on the curve. The spline moves towards each of the control points but never touches them. The more control points, the more pull exerted on the curve. The spline may cross the control frame, but it never meets the frame.

This type of spline is called a B-spline. AutoCAD permits two types of B-spline curves: quadratic and cubic (cubic is the default.) The system variable **splinetype** controls whether the spline output is quadratic or cubic:

```
SPLINETYPE set to 5 =
    Quadratic
SPLINETYPE set to 6 = Cubic
```

99

Splines can be modified after the fact with DDMODIFY. Let's use DDMODIFY (Modify toolbar, Properties option) to change our spline to quadratic and we'll review the difference between these two splines.

Quadratic splines are easier to predict. Notice that the curve hits the midpoint of each side of the control frame. Quadratic splines are generated using a lower order of equation than cubic splines.

The system variable **splinesegs** controls the number of polyline segments between vertices of the control frame. The default is 8, which indicates 8 polyline segments from one control point to another. The higher this value, the smoother the curve. Setting the value too high could dramatically decrease the speed at which the curve is generated, because it adds so much data to the drawing. Setting the value too low results in a rougher spline result. If you want to change the spline segment setting of existing splines, change the **splinesegs** value and respline the curve (PEDIT command). There's no need to decurve the spline first.

If you set **splinesegs** to a negative value (-8) AutoCAD will generate arc segments rather than line segments, which will also generate some very nice polysplines. The resulting spline looks the same and differences will only be noticed when editing or object snapping.

## Editing Polysplines

Editing a spline can lead to mixed results. Commands like MOVE, ERASE, COPY, ROTATE, and so on act on both the control frame and the spline (whether the frame is visible or not). These editing operations leave the frame intact. Commands such as BREAK and TRIM delete the control frame and leave you the resulting spline curve. The curve fitting becomes permanent and it can no longer be edited in PEDIT. OFFSET generates another spline (without a frame). STRETCHing a polyspline actually stretches the control frame, and recalculates the spline using the new modified frame. The Join option in the PEDIT command automatically decurves the spline to join another contiguous pline to the frame. You would need to manually spline the frame again. Commands such as DIVIDE, MEASURE, and FILLET ignore the frame and work on the spline only. The same is true of Object Snap modes.

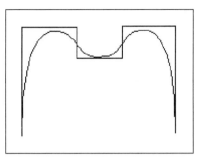

**Figure 3:** Cubic spline curve.

If you use a linetype other than continuous, you'll need to be sure the system variable **plinegen** is set to 1. This ensures that AutoCAD views the spline as one continuous entity rather than many small pline segments. The option **Ltype gen** in the PEDIT command can be used to modify existing splines.

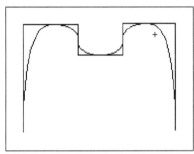

**Figure 4:** Quadradic spline curve.

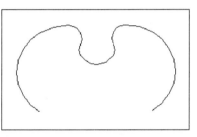

**Figure 5:** Fit curve.

Entity grips work great with splines. The grips display on the vertices of the control frame and you can easily change the resulting spline on the fly. I strongly suggest you use grips to modify a spline rather than trying to use the Edit Vertex options in PEDIT.

Using the same spline, reenter the DDMODIFY command and select Fit Curve. Notice the unexpected results?

Fit curves are made up of actual polyarcs. The curve fits all the vertices. This curve is made up of a pair of arcs joining each pair of vertices. A control frame, such as the one we've chosen, is too dramatic to achieve good results with the Fit Curve option. A good control frame would consist of a gradual shift in direction with many more control points. Notice that the original frame is gone. You can control the fit curve within the PEDIT command using the Tangent option (under Edit vertex). This process is so incredibly tedious and difficult to control that I'm not even going to cover it.

Fit curves maintain accuracy. You know a Fit Curve will travel through every vertex. Those creating topol maps, where accuracy is of chief importance, would never use spline curves because the integrity of their drawings would be lost. In this case, Fit Curve would be the better choice.

Fit curves are not allowed to enter the 3D world of AutoCAD because they're made up of arcs. Polysplines however, because they're linear, fit nicely into the 3D world (all releases that support splines). To generate a 3D polyspline you need to use the 3DPOLY command to create a control frame. Using the previously described procedure, you'll enter PEDIT and spline the frame. The Fit Curve option doesn't even exist when editing a **3dpoly**. You can not set **splinesegs** to a negative number to generate arcs rather than line segments when creating a 3D spline:

```
Command: PEDIT
Select Polyline: select a
   3DPOLY
Close/Edit vertex/Spline curve/Decurve/Undo/eXit<X>:
```

Notice how many options are missing when you select a 3D polyline. To get true 3D curves, you need to use newer NURBS-based splines.

Ellipses need little explanation, but in preparation for the next chapter let's quickly review. A Release 12 ellipse is made up of a combination of many polyarcs. An ellipse is not a defined object within AutoCAD until Release 13. If you list out a Release 12 ellipse, you'll find it listed as a polyline. It is nearly impossible to find the center or quadrants of a Release 12 ellipse. Object snaps grab the geometry of each individual polyarc, and not the ellipse as a whole. There are two methods of creating an ellipse:

- Define the center, one axis endpoint, and the distance of the other axis.
- Define one axis (picking two endpoints) and the other axis distance. In the pull-down menu this is displayed as Axis, eccentricity. It doesn't matter whether you select the major or the minor axis first.

Both of the previous options also permit defining the rotation about the major axis:

```
Command: ELLIPSE
Center/<Axis endpoint 1>:
    pick one axis endpoint
Axis endpoint 2:pick the
    other axis endpoint
<Other axis distance>/
    Rotation:
```

When selecting the "other axis distance," you're literally defining only the distance. By this point, the direction of the ellipse has already been established. The Rotation option is used to define the rotation about the major axis. Valid angles range from 0 to 89.4 degrees. A value of 0 generates a circle while a value of 89.4 creates an ellipse that is nearly a line. In geometric terms, an ellipse with a rotation angle of 90 would generate a line. Therefore, AutoCAD won't allow us to input any value over 89.4.

If isometric mode is on, an additional option will appear in the ELLIPSE command, called Isocircle. The ELLIPSE command can also be used to generate circles that are rotated according to the current isometric plane. The end result is still an ellipse, however.

# Splines and Ellipses

The new NURBS-based curves introduced in Release 13 were a welcome addition. No more makeshift ellipses or splines—now we can have the real thing. The ellipses and splines of previous AutoCAD versions were merely approximations, comprised of polyline and polyarc segments. Manipulating the segments or grabbing key geometric points was difficult. Now AutoCAD incorporates NURBS mathematics and algorithms into its functionality to generate true ellipses and splines. These ellipses and splines also use less disk space and memory than the polylines of previous releases.

NURBS stands for Nonuniform Rational Basis Spline (which we simply call B-splines). The fact that these splines are nonuniform permits the uneven spacing of knots, should you need to create a very sharp curve. Rational permits combining regular geometry, such as arcs and ellipses, with the irregular free-form curves. B-spline refers to the precise curve-fitting ability generated from data points (thanks to Bezier).

The ELLIPSE command of Release 13 and 14 looks almost identical to that of previous releases. Drawing the new NURBS-based ellipse should be completely transparent. Using our past method, let's create a couple of ellipses:

```
Command: ELLIPSE
Arc/Center/<Axis endpoint 1>: pick one axis endpoint
Axis endpoint 2: pick the second
<Other axis distance>/Rotation: select the other axis dis-
  tance
```

The command sequence is identical to the one used in Release 12. The resulting ellipse, however, is mathematically accurate and contains valuable geometric information. Did you ever try to find the center of an ellipse? How about a quadrant? Now, that's no problem. Note the grip points on a Release 12 ellipse versus those on the new NURBS-based ellipse, as shown in Figure 1.

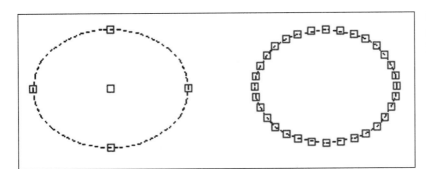

**Figure 1:** Entity grips on Release 13 versus Release 12.

The new system variable pellipse can be set to 1 to use the old Release 12 ellipse.

The new ELLIPSE command still has the Center, Axis, and Rotation option from the old ELLIPSE command. A new option, Arc, has been added. This option is used to create elliptical arcs, which was done in Release 12 by generating an entire ellipse and trimming it down to an arc. This new method eliminates a tedious editing step. When creating an elliptical arc, you first define an entire ellipse, then indicate the starting and ending points of the desired arc:

```
Command: ellipse
Arc/Center/<Axis endpoint 1>: a
<Axis endpoint 1>/Center: pick one axis endpoint
Axis endpoint 2: pick the other axis endpoint
```

```
<Other axis distance>/Rotation:
Parameter/<start angle>: pick the starting point of the
    arc
Parameter/Included/<end angle>: pick the endpoint of the
    arc
```

You can also select an included angle after specifying the starting point of the elliptical arc. The Parameter option, shown in Figure 2, is quite difficult to interpret and even more difficult to explain. This option was derived from basic drafting practices for creating an ellipse or elliptical arc. Let's review the Parameter option:

```
Command: ellipse
Arc/Center/<Axis endpoint 1>: a
<Axis endpoint 1>/Center:
Axis endpoint 2:
<Other axis distance>/Rotation:
Parameter/<start angle>: p
Angle/<start parameter>:
Angle/Included/<end parameter>:
```

**Figure 2:** The Arc, parameter options and the Elipse command.

As before, we first define an ellipse and then define the part of the ellipse we want to keep (our arc). Imagine a circle drawn with the same diameter as the major axis of the ellipse, as shown in Figure 2. Select the two points on this imaginary circle as previously indicated, to define two parameters. AutoCAD drops two perpendicular projections into the ellipse to determine the length of the final elliptical arc. You will rarely need to create this type of ellipse, but because it's not defined in the *User Refer-*

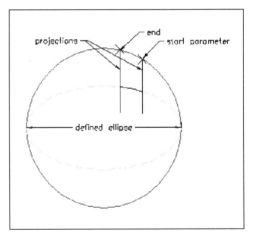

*ence Manual,* I thought it would be helpful to define it here. Those of you who started on drafting boards should find this procedure familiar, while those who began with CAD will no doubt find this option of little use.

The Isocircle option from previous releases remains in the new ELLIPSE command. When set to isometric drawing mode (SNAP command, Style option) the command sequence for ELLIPSE is modified to include the Isocircle option. When selected, AutoCAD will draw isocircles with a desired location and radius parallel to the current isometric plane. This procedure is 2D only, and simply gives the appearance of 3D:

```
Command: ellipse
Arc/Center/Isocircle/<Axis endpoint 1>:
Axis endpoint 2:
<Other axis distance>/Rotation:
```

After constructing an ellipse or two, notice how easy it is to edit with grips. The new ellipses accept object snaps (center and quadrant) as well. (Words of warning: if you offset an ellipse, you get a spline, which is mathematically accurate.)

## Splines

The new NURBS curvescan be confusing and somewhat intimidating at first, but with practice and some basic information, you'll be splining in no time. The new NURB spline is a fourth-order curve but can be elevated using the SPLINEDIT command.

As you create a spline (with the SPLINE command), you define datapoints. AutoCAD fits the spline to the data points. The final step is defining the spline's tangency constraints (optional). Let's review the basic prompt sequence for creating a NURB spline:

```
Command: spline
Object/<Enter first point>:
Enter point:
Close/Fit Tolerance/<Enter point>:
```

```
Close/Fit Tolerance/<Enter point>:
Close/Fit Tolerance/<Enter point>: enter
Enter start tangent:
Enter end tangent:
```

Select a series of points creating a figure similar to an M. Notice how the spline travels through each of the data points you are selecting. When you're finished selecting points, hit <Enter>. You will be asked to select a new starting tangent constraint and an ending tangent, defined by a vector located at your cursor, connecting to the starting or ending points of the curve. As you spin this tangent vector, notice the changes that take place on your spline.

Should you want to leave the curve as it was originally defined, hit <Enter>. Accepting the defaults will create a smooth curve with "C2 continuity." A curve such as this has no sudden changes in the curvature of the spline.

The SPLINE command has a few defaults that need addressing: Object, Close, and Fit tolerance.

Perhaps you want to take an existing Release 12 spline comprised of polyarcs and convert it into the new NURB splines in Release 13. Select the Object option of the SPLINE command (even though you might have expected to find this capability in the SPLINEDIT command). The order of the spline is preserved. If you recall, two types of splines were available in Release 12: cubic and quadratic. The cubic splines were fourth order and quadratic were third. If you convert a quadratic spline to the new NURBS-based spline in Release 13, it will maintain an order of three.

The Close option creates a closed spline. You will still be asked for a tangency constraint. If you were to List a closed spline, you'd find that closed splines are "periodic," while open splines are considered "nonperiodic."

The Fit tolerance option controls how closely the spline fits the data points. A tolerance value of zero (the default setting) draws the spline directly through each of the data points. As you increase the value of the tolerance, you'll notice the curve pull away from the data points. Figure 3 is an illustration of the dramatic difference a tolerance value can create.

The options may lead you to think you can have different tolerance values for different parts of the spline, which is not true. It doesn't matter at what point you change the tolerance value because the set-ting affects the entire spline.

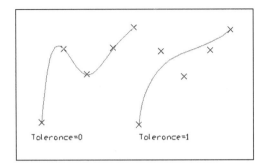

**Figure 3:** Using the Fit Tolerance option you can establish the degree to which the spline follows the data points.

## Editing splines

Using entity grips is the easiest method of editing a spline. Through grips, you can stretch a spline through the data points to make minor modifications. Major and more detailed modifi-cations to a spline must be done through the SPLINEDIT command.

The SPLINEDIT command permits editing of the actual spline (using the previously defined data points) or the control frame. A Bezier control frame is associated with every spline. To see this frame, we need to turn the system variable splframe on (set to 1) and regenerate the drawing, as shown in Figure 4. As soon as you enter the SPLINEDIT command, you'll see grips appear on the control frame—not on the spline, as you might expect. Let's review the SPLINEDIT command:

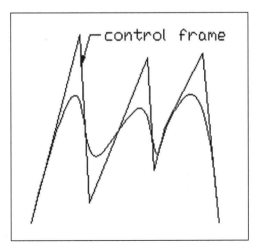

**Figure 4:** A Bezier control frame is asso-ciated with every spline.

109

```
Command: splinedit
Select spline:
Fit Data/Close/Move Vertex/Refine/rEverse/Undo/eXit <X>:
```

To edit the spline directly, choose Fit Data (for data points). The grips will appear on the spline, and you'll encounter an entirely new list of options.

## Add/Close/Open/Delete/Move

Add adds more data points to the spline. You select the existing data point (now a grip) that you want to add a data point after. The grip selected and the next grip will turn red. You can now select the position of the new data point. You can continue adding data points between the two highlighted grips or select another data point to work from. Adding data points could change the existing spline.

Close closes an open spline (it doesn't appear as an option if the spline is already closed). The tangent becomes continuous (smooth) at its endpoints.

Open opens a closed spline (it doesn't appear as an option if the spline is already open). If the spline was previously closed in the SPLINEDIT command, it returns the spline to its original state.

Delete removes data fit points and recalculates the spline.

Move is similar to the PEDIT command in that it moves existing data points. You're unable to pick the desired grip but must step through all of them to get to the data point you want to move. Additional options will appear to assist you in this process.

## Purge/Tangents/Tolerance/Exit

Purge removes all fit data points, leaving you with only the control frame to work with. You are returned to the main SPLINEDIT prompts and the Fit Data option is removed from the command sequence. Though you can undo immediately to bring the Fit Data information back, there isn't a command option to restore these data points, so choose this option carefully.

Tangents permit you to modify the start and end tangents of the spline. If the spline is closed, you'll only be prompted for one tangent. You can use the Tangent or Perpendicular object snaps to snap to other objects, if necessary.

Tolerance permits you to change the existing tolerance value for the spline. Exit returns you to the main SPLINEDIT options.

All of these options are a subset of the Fit Data option. As you can see, the SPLINEDIT command can become overwhelming due to the number of options. Let's return to the main SPLINEDIT options in an effort to clear up the confusion.

## Fit Data/Close/Move Vertex/Refine

Close is the same as the Close option in the Fit Data options. This option closes an open spline.

Open opens a closed spline. I've noticed that Open works somewhat differently than the Open in the Fit Data options. When I opened a spline I had closed in SPLINEDIT, it removed the starting segment rather than the closing segment. I expected my spline to be returned to its original state.

Move Vertex relocates the selected control points. You have to step through the vertices to get the desired grip. Additional prompts will be provided to facilitate this function.

Refine provides an additional tool to fine-tune your spline. Let's review the suboptions.

## Add Control Point/Elevate Order/Weight

Add Control Point increases the number of control points on the control frame. This option is easier than the Add option under Fit Data. Simply select a point on the screen, and the spline will recalculate accordingly.

With Elevate Order, splines are created as fourth-order equations (lines are second order, circles and arcs are third). You can elevate the order and increase the number of control points accordingly. The highest order permitted is 26. As you elevate the order, you cannot go backwards (mathematically

111

impossible). If you change the equation to eighth order, you can not reduce it to sixth. Elevating the order permits more localized control of the spline.

Weight allows you to weight the various control points. Weight references the distance between the control point and the actual spline. The larger the value (integer only), the more the spline is pulled toward the selected control point. Once you weight the spline, AutoCAD makes it rational. The default value is one.

The SPLINEDIT command is filled with more options than you'll ever need. Experimenting with the command will help you feel more comfortable modifying your splines. Despite the number of options available with the SPLINEDIT command, it is not too complicated to work with.

Now you're a NURBS expert. Enjoy the new ellipses and splines as you incorporate them into your AutoCAD drawings.

# The Aerial
# Viewer

T he mysterious aerial view (aka DSVIEWER) was introduced with AutoCAD Release 12 for Windows, and
although it took some effort to figure out and get comfortable with, it was a great asset to the program. **Aerial view**
gave us the ability to see our drawings in their entirety, and
zoom in and out without any dreaded regenerations. Before
Release 12, the magnification and navigation tools found in
DSVIEWER were only available through third-party software or
expensive graphics cards.

This chapter will explore the DSVIEWER command in both
Release 12 and 14. Once you familiarize yourself with this
command, you'll find many ways to use it. Though rather cumbersome at first, DSVIEWER could become your best friend in no time.

Just remember, regenerations are the enemy. DSVIEWER will
rescue you from needless regens. DSVIEWER is also definitely a
step-above the dynamic view option in the ZOOM command
(though not as cool as RTPAN and RTZOOM). Release 12 users
should definitely listen up!

## Release 12

The Release 12 DSVIEWER icon has puzzled many users
(including myself). The aerial view icon lives along the status
line by default in Release 12.

There are a few aerial view rules:

- It can't be used while in Paper Space.
- It can't be used when Perspective Mode is on.
- You must be configured for the Windows accelerated display driver with the display-list option (the default).
- It does not work when Fast Zoom mode is off (the VIEWRES command).

Open an existing drawing and select the aerial view icon. The aerial view window will appear in the lower right-hand corner. You will see a global view of your drawing within this window. As you Zoom and Pan within this window, you will see your drawing update; to prepare for this, you need to ensure that your DSVIEWER toggles are set properly.

**Figure 1:** R12 aerial view window.

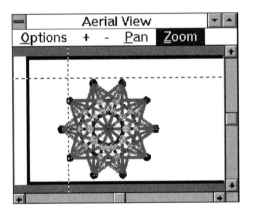

Notice the five options across the top of the aerial view window, shown in figure 1: Options, plus (+), minus (-), Pan, and Zoom. Select the Options menu and make sure the following toggles are ON or checked.

## Window on Top Dynamic Update

Since we will be using aerial view primarily for panning and zooming, let's start there. Aerial view is either in Zoom mode or Pan mode. The current mode is controlled by selecting from the aerial view menu bar. Select Zoom and select the two corners of a window in the aerial view drawing area. This will change the display of the entire drawing while keeping your aerial view window intact. Notice the rectangle displayed within the Aerial View window. This rectangle indicates your Zoom window.

To pan, select Pan mode from the aerial view menu bar. The Pan box will appear. Use this box to relocate the display without changing the magnification. Move the Pan box to a new location and pick.

Notice the scroll bars in the aerial view window. As you scroll from right to left and top to bottom you'll see the aerial view display move accordingly. This action does not affect the drawing display.

On the aerial view menu bar you'll also see plus (+) and plus (-). These options control the magnification of the aerial view display. Plus will double the current magnification, and minus will cut the magnification in half (zoom out). Neither one of these two options will affect the drawing display. Let's review the Options menu again.

## Global View

As you change the view within the aerial view window, you can use global view to redisplay the entire drawing. This does not affect the actual drawing display.

## Locate

Locate is definitely my favorite option. If you've ever searched endlessly through your drawing in search of some minute detail, you'll love this option. **Locate** let's you move your cursor around your actual drawing display while showing a magnified view of each section within the aerial view window.

Be sure you're zoomed out in your actual drawing display. Select the locate option. Move your cursor (which now becomes small crosshairs) around in the drawing display (not the aerial view display). Notice the magnified view within the aerial view window. To change the actual drawing display to match the drawing display, simply pick.

Locate defaults to a magnification of eight times the view. To change this magnification click the right mouse button while using locate, which will display the magnification dialog box.

Minus and plus decrease and increase the magnification respectively (though 8 is a good default).

## Statistics

Statistics provides information about the display list driver.

## AutoViewport

**AutoViewport** is tricky. This option only comes into play if you're using paper space (remember DSVIEWER doesn't work in Paper Space!). If you have multiple viewports in Paper Space and you're currently in Model Space, AutoViewport could be important. When toggled on, you can bounce from viewport to viewport and change the viewport display using aerial view. When toggled off, aerial view will affect the original current viewport only, even if you change the current viewport while in DSVIEWER. This is ON by default and I suggest you leave it that way.

## Window on Top

When toggled on, the aerial view window remains on top until manually closed. When off, the aerial view window is on top for one operation and then closed automatically (the default is ON).

## Dynamic Update

When toggled ON, the aerial view window display is updated as you update the drawing. On complex edits, this could substantially slow you down.

The AERIAL VIEW command (DSVIEWER) is transparent and can be executed while in another command. Tip: double-clicking on Zoom will do a Zoom on the entire drawing display.

## Release 14

For starters, the aerial view icon resembles an airplane—some-

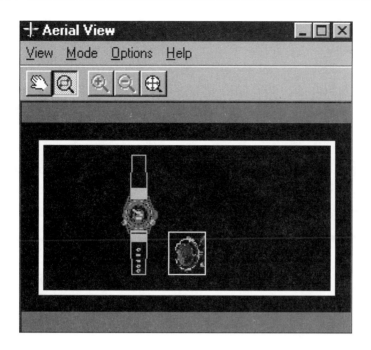

**Figure 2:** Aerial view, Release 14.

thing I would actually associate with an aerial view. The aerial view tool resides on the Standard toolbar.

The DSVIEWER command works much the same in Release 14. We have icons instead of words for consistency with the user interface. Like Release 12, aerial views do not work in Paper Space, perspective views, or when Fast Zoom mode is off.

Open an existing drawing and execute the DSVIEWER command. The aerial view window will display the entire drawing. Across the top of the aerial view menu bar are four pull-downs on top of five tools. All the tool icons have tooltips attached to them. We'll start with the tools from left to right.

The first tool (with an icon that looks like a hand) enters Pan mode much the same as Release 12. You can pan the drawing by moving the view box (without changing the magnification).

The zoom tool (magnifying glass icon) permits selecting a Zoom window. Where Release 12 requires two picks on the window, Release 14 operates via a pick and drag to form the window.

You'll notice the locator button is missing in Release 14 (which was my favorite part of the Aerial viewer).

The third tool across zooms in (+); the fourth tool zooms out (-); and the fifth tool (Global) displays the entire drawing within the aerial view window. None of these tools change the actual drawing display.

The last three options are the same as in Release 12— **AutoViewport**, **Dynamic Update**, and **Display Statistics**.

Aerial view is a great method of zooming and panning with very little effort. Don't waste your time regenerating your drawing needlessly by zooming in and out to get to your desired view—use the DSVIEWER command and optimize your display efforts.

# New Dimensioning Techniques

The new dimensioning features that appeared first in Release 13 are some of the best additions to AutoCAD. The old Dim prompt has been cast by the wayside and replaced with new streamlined dimensioning commands. Third-party developers and programmers are delighted because it makes programming much easier. The Dim roadblock has been removed, and users will love the timesavings the new Inference dimensioning lends. The new DDIM dialog box is easy to understand and takes the pain out of setting dimension variables.

The old **dim** commands are still available so those who have written routines that address old dimensioning practices have no need to panic. The new commands reside at the Command prompt. In some cases many commands have been folded into one. Table 1 shows a list of old commands and their new equivalents.

Some of these commands are long but there's nothing to keep you from aliasing them in the ACAD.PGP file (which I would recommend you do immediately). The new command equivalents are listed with the minimum acceptable input in uppercase. For example, you don't have to key in the entire **dimdiameter** command, **dimdia** will suffice. I always use the Dimension toolbar when I know I'm going to be investing time in dimensioning as seen in Figure 1. You can also find all of the dimensioning commands in the Dimension pull-down menu. Let's review the new dimensioning procedures:

**Table 1:** Old dim commands and their new equivalents.

| Old DIM Command | New Command Equivalent |
| --- | --- |
| ALIGNED | DIMALIgned |
| BASELINE | DIMBASEline |
| CONTINUE | DIMCONTinue |
| HORIZONTAL | DIMLINear |
| ROTATED | DIMLINear |
| VERTICAL | DIMLINear |
| ANGULAR | DIMANGular |
| CENTER | DIMCENTER |
| DIAMETER | DIMDIAmeter |
| RADIUS | DIMRADius |
| ORDINATE | DIMORDinate |
| LEADER | LEADer |
| HOMETEXT | DIMEDit |
| NEWTEXT | DIMEDit |
| OBLIQUE | DIMEDit |
| TROTATE | DIMEDit |
| TEDIT | DIMTEDit |
| RESTORE | DIMSTYle |
| SAVE | DIMSTYle |
| STATUS | DIMSTYle |
| UPDATE | DIMSTYle (apply option) |
| VARIABLE | DIMSTYle |
| OVERRIDE | DIMOVERride |

**Figure 1:** Dimension toolbar.

```
   At the Command: prompt, enter the DIMLINEAR command.
Command: DIMLINEAR
First extension line origin or press enter to select:
```

Hit <Enter> to select. Select any diagonal line entity in your drawing. You'll see inference dimensioning kick in as you pull the dimension up, down, and across. As you pull the dimension line up, AutoCAD will assume you want horizontal dimension-

ing. As you pull the dimension line to the left or right, Auto-
CAD will assume vertical dimensioning. If you select a point on
the screen, AutoCAD will place your dimension using the
desired location. AutoCAD will assume you want to accept the
default dimension text value. This **dimlinear** command eliminates two tedious steps from previous releases: having to
indicate horizontal or vertical, and having to hit <Enter> to
accept the default text value. What if you want to change your
text value? What if AutoCAD assumed horizontal and you
really wanted vertical? Before you place your dimension in its
final location, let's review the options available for dimension
line location (Text/Angle/Horizontal/ Vertical/Rotated):

- Text option is used to specify another value. Be aware that
  once you input another value, the dimension text is no
  longer associative.
- Angle permits changing the dimension text angle.
- Horizontal and Vertical is used to override inference
  dimensioning and force a particular type of dimensioning.
- Rotated is used to create rotated linear dimensions.

**Dimaligned** is its own stand-alone command. Use this command for diagonal lines. The procedure and options (Text/Angle)
follow the same rules as **dimlinear**.

**Dimangular** has been streamlined—the command no longer
prompts you for text position. **Dimangular** assumes you want
to center the dimension text along the dimension line arc. If you
want to modify **dimangular**'s position, use grips or **dimedit**.

**Dimdia**, **dimrad**, and **dimord** work exactly the same as
before. **Dimcontinue** and **dimbaseline** have been optimized
for greater efficiency as well.

```
Command: DIMCONT
Specify a second extension line origin or (Undo/<Select>):
```

Continue and Baseline dimensions in Release 12 allowed the
creation of one dimension only. To create another dimension,
you had to re-enter the command. Release 12 also prompted

you for text. If you were creating many baseline or continue dimensions, this prompting quickly became tedious. Release 13 and 14 continually prompt for the next dimension to continue without leaving the **dimcontinue** command. You can also select another base dimension in the middle of the command. You could feasibly place all continued dimensions in your drawing without ever leaving the **dimcontinue** command. The same is true for the **dimbaseline** command.

In addition, AutoCAD now supports continued Angular, Aligned, Rotated, and Ordinate dimensions (baseline where applicable). When continuing ordinate dimensions, AutoCAD will bend the dimension line if necessary to avoid a collision with the previous drawn dimension line.

**Dimedit** streamlined many dimensioning commands into one:

```
Command: DIMEDIT
Dimension Edit
 (Home/New/Rotate/Oblique):
```

This command can be used to recenter the dimension text (Home), modify the value of dimension text (New), Rotate multiple dimension text strings, and Oblique the angle of the dimension lines (for isometric dimensioning). The new **dimtedit** command is exactly as the tedit command was in Release 12.

Leader dimensions of the past have avoided the associative world of dimensioning. Erasing a leader in Release 12 meant erasing the individual arrowhead, leader lines, and text. Release 13 and 14 has finally pulled dimension leaders into the realm of associativity. Leaders can be updated later to reflect the current settings of dimension variables.

The new **leader** command also provides the means to create curved leader lines (which I've been asked about on many occasions). Using the new NURBS based geometry, splines are now a **leader** option. Leaders may now have several lines of text attached to the leader, thanks to the new Mtext faciity. Let's review the new leader command:

```
Command: LEADER
From point: pick the point for the arrowhead
To point: pick vertex
To point (Format/Annotation/Undo) <Annotation>: enter
Annotation (or RETURN for options): enter dimension text
```

AutoCAD will automatically draw a hook line if the angle of the leader line is greater than 15 degrees from the horizontal.

The Format options consist of Spline/Straight/Arrow/None. Spline implements the new spline curve discussed earlier. Straight draws the standard leader lines. None draws a leader with no arrow, Arrow restores the arrowhead. This procedure is demonstrated in Figure 2.

Annotation controls a variety of text options, including Tolerance/Copy/Block/None/<Mtext>.

Tolerance enters the realm of geometric dimensioning and tolerancing (GD&T). This option will place a GD&T dimension at the end of the leader line. Copy is used to copy an existing object in the drawing and place it at the end of the leader line. The acceptable objects are limited to text, mtext, a GD&T dimension, or a block. This option is great for balloon callouts and duplicating existing leader text.

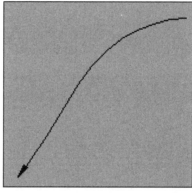

**Figure 2:** Splined leader.

The Block option will prompt for an existing block name and insert it at the end of the leader line. The options are the same as those in the **insert** command, so you can modify the scale factor and rotation angle before it's placed in the drawing. AutoCAD will not display a hook line when using this option. Should you want a leader line with no dimension text, select the None option.

The Annotation Mtext option allows multiline text at the end of your leader line. Simply draw the two opposite corners of the text rectangle and AutoCAD will use this as a bounding box to determine the length of the lines. The text will be offset from the hook line by the current dimgap value. The height of the text is controlled by the **dimtxt** variable. After selecting the rectangle, you'll be sent to the mtext dialog box for inputting the dimension text. If you're on the DOS platform, you'll be shelled out of AutoCAD to the Edit editor. The Windows platform has its own editor within the AutoCAD program.

Because the **leader** command creates a true Mtext object, you can edit it as you would any Mtext object. If it's important that the dimension text appear above the hook line, set **dimtad** to On (Text Above Dimension line).

If you find the LEADER command too complicated, you might try the new Quick Leader command in the bonus toolbars (Release 14). This will send you to a nice dialog box that makes it easier to view the results of your leader line.

Take a look at the dimension-style dialog box (Ddim) as seen in Figure 3. DDIM not only incorporates icons into the dialog box (officially referred to as image tiles), but these image tiles

**Figure 3:** Dimension Styles dialog box.

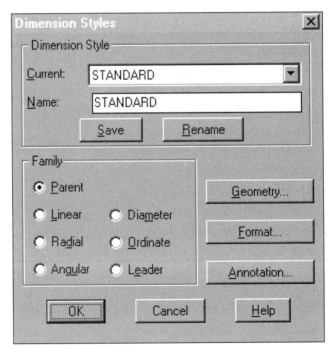

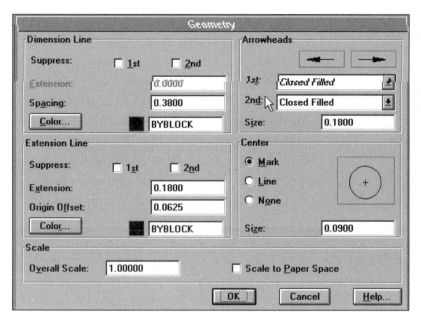

**Figure 4:** The Geometry subdialog box contains the setting for the physical appearance of the dimension and the overall scale factor.

have intelligence. If you select on the image tile—it toggles through a variety of settings. Each click changes the current settings and shows you the end dimensioning result. DDIM has streamlined the dialog box into three categories: Geometry, Format, and Annotation.

The Geometry subdialog box contains the setting for the physical appearance of the dimension and the overall scale factor. It's within this dialog box that you could dynamically change the arrowheads, center lines, or suppress the extension lines. Two dimension variables, **dimsd1** and **dimsd2**, have been added to this section. **Dimsd1** suppresses the first dimension line up to the text, **dimsd2** suppresses the second. These settings will come into play when dimension text is placed outside the extension lines, as shown in Figure 4.

The Format subdialog box controls the location of dimension text, arrowheads, leader lines, and dimension lines. The image tiles make the selection process painless. A new Japanese Industrial standard (JIS) has been added to the vertical justification options. Selecting the User Defined checkbox adds great flexibility to your text placement (another improvement over Release 12).

125

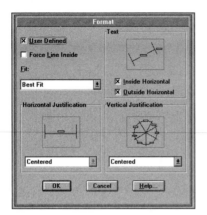

As you select the dimension line placement, you'll also be selecting where you'd like the text to be placed. I'd highly recommend this option for those of you who are constantly moving the dimension text. Two new variables, **dimfit** and **dimjust**, are also included in this box. **Dimfit** controls the end result when text doesn't fit within the extension lines, **dimjust** controls the new placement options of horizontal text, as shown in Figure 5.

**Figure 5:** The format subdialog box controls the location of dimension text, arrowheads, leader lines, and dimension lines.

The Annotation subdialog box controls the dimension text settings as seen in Figure 6. A new Units setting for dimensions only has been added, which lets you maintain a different precision value while drawing than you would for dimensioning. This dialog box also has image tiles for controlling tolerances, limits, and basic dimensioning.

**Figure 6:** Annotation dialog box.

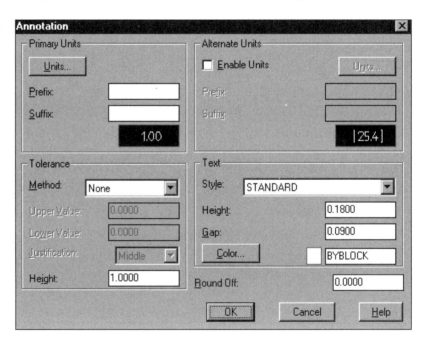

# Dimension Style Families

Dimension styles, introduced with Release 11 of Auto-CAD, were intended to revolutionize dimensioning practices. However, the inflexibility of these styles and the cumbersome user interface caused many people to ignore their existence. The concept was good, but the implementation needed help. Release 13 took this concept and expanded on it to make it easier and more logical. Let's take a look at dimension style families and their children.

Prior to Release 13, you were forced to set up a completely different dimension style to accommodate dimension variable settings for linear dimensioning, which varies from the settings for diameter or radius. Dimension families permit setting dimension variables according to dimension type: linear, diameter, radius, angular, ordinate, and leader.

The average AutoCAD user has been forced to use dimension styles since Release 11. Even if you didn't intend to create a dimension style, it was created for you. A mystery style by the name of Unnamed existed, and was constantly being updated. Release 13 got rid of this mystery style, starting off with a default style called Standard, which adds consistency to the default text and mline style names of Standard.

## The Dimensioning Begins

Let's assume total dimension style ignorance for a moment. In general, you set up your dimension variables the way you like them, then save them to a style. If you have several different settings, you'll be using them to create several different styles. You may want to create one style with tolerances, one without, one with arrowheads, one with dots, and so on. Basically, you assign a different name to each style.

Due to the intelligent "inference" dimensioning, AutoCAD can distinguish between different types of dimensions. This added intelligence includes the obvious ability to assign different variable settings to the different types of dimensions, without creating an entirely new style. Think of this process as one tree with many branches.

Open the Ddim dialog box and notice the distinction between the Parent and Child dimension style settings as seen in Figure 1. The children refer to the individual types mentioned above: linear, angular, diameter, radial, ordinate, and leader. If you want

**Figure 1:** Dimension Styles dialog box.

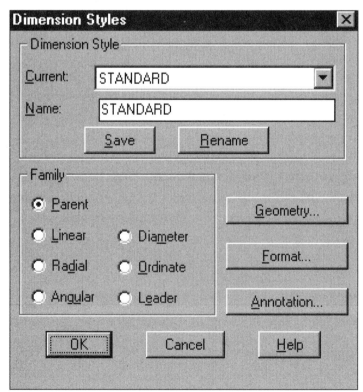

a dimension variable to reflect all your dimensions, regardless of type, you'll assign it to the Parent setting. If you want a dimension variable setting to affect only one type of dimension, select that particular dimension type (Child), change the variables, and save the modifications. Each time you make changes to either the Child or Parent, you must pick save to update the style. Failure to save will result in creating an Override, which we'll discuss later.

While in the Ddim dialog box, we'll create a style called Sample. Type Sample next to the Name option and save it. This procedure will make a copy of the current Standard style settings but assign it to a new name. Be certain that Parent is selected, and pick the Annotation subdialog box. Change the color of the dimension text to yellow. Pick OK to exit the Annotation dialog box and pick Save to save the change to our Sample dimension style. Because you assigned this to the Parent, all our text will be yellow regardless of the type of dimension.

Now we'll assign some different variable settings to a child. Select Linear, then go to the Geometry subdialog box. Change the arrowheads to dots. Save this setting to our dimension style Sample. Whenever you draw a linear dimension, you get dots. Select Diameter and change the color of the text (the Annotation subdialog box again) to cyan. Save this setting to Sample as well. We've just defined a Sample style and two children. The other children will only incorporate the settings of the parent.

Draw a linear dimension (aligned, horizontal, vertical, or rotated). You'll notice that the text is yellow (because of the Parent) and you will have dots instead of arrowheads (because of the Child settings). Draw a diameter dimension (you'll probably need a circle). Notice you are back to arrowheads but the text is cyan (you overrode the parent setting of dimension text color). Try angular or radius, the dimension text will be yellow to follow the parent.

Note that AutoCAD stores all the dimensioning system variables to a style name except for two—**dimsho** and **dimaso**. These two variables must be set at the command prompt and will not be assigned to the current dimension style. **Dimsho** controls whether dynamic dragging is on while editing and inserting dimensions. **Dimaso** turns associative dimensioning on or off (thou shalt never turn **dimaso** off).

What happens if you change the settings that belong to the Sample dimension style? Will it affect existing dimensions? Return to the Ddim dialog box (it should be in Parent mode). Go to the Annotation subdialog box and select Basic dimensioning (by the Tolerance method). This process will draw a box around your dimension text. Save this setting to Sample and exit the dialog. Did your existing dimensions update? Now you've seen how you can control your dimensions with dimension styles.

## Creating Overrides

What if you want to change some dimension variable settings but don't want to affect the existing dimensions? You could create an entirely new dimension style. What if you just want to quickly change some variables for one or two unusual dimensions you're about to create. It's hardly worth storing these dimension settings by assigning them to a style. You can create an Override. Overrides only affect those dimensions to come. You may also set up overrides and hand select the dimensions you want to modify (rather than all of them). Let's set up some overrides.

Return to the Ddim dialog box. Let's change our arrowheads to tick marks (Geometry subdialog box). Feel free to make other modifications as well. Do not save this to the dimension style, simply pick Ok to exit the dialog box. You have just created an override. Your existing dimensions should remain intact. Any new dimensions will have tick marks instead of arrowheads regardless of the type of dimension drawn.

If you return to the Ddim dialog box, you'll see the dimension style name has changed to +Sample. The + indicates you have one or more override set.

If you want to apply these overrides to any of your existing dimensions, you can use the **dimstyle** command. When entering the **dimstyle** command you'll see this:

```
Command: DIMSTYLE
Current dimension style: SAMPLE
Dimension variable overrides:

DIMBLK1: OBLIQUE
DIMBLK2: OBLIQUE
DIMSAH: On

?/Save/STatus/Variables/Apply/<Restore>: Apply
(select the dimensions you wish updated).
```

The other options in the dimstyle command yield basically the same results as the **ddim** command at the command level (for those who just can't bear to use dialog boxes).
- Save: saves the current dimension variable settings to a dimension style.
- STatus: displays the current dimension variables settings.
- Restore: restores a predefined dimension style.
- Variables: display the variable settings of any dimension.
- ?: will list any existing dimension styles.

In our case we'd see:

```
STANDARD
SAMPLE
SAMPLE$0
SAMPLE$4
```

The Parent style Sample has two children, Sample$0 and Sample$4. The zero value is a linear child, the four is a diameter child. I admit that this syntax is somewhat hostile, but it's easy once you crack the code. Other children settings include:

```
$0 linear
$2 angular
$3 radius
```

```
$4 diameter
$6 ordinate
$7 leader
```

You can compare two different dimension styles in the **dimstyle** command as well. To compare the difference between the Standard and Sample dimension styles use the Variables option coupled with the tilde (~):

```
?/Enter dimension style name or RETURN to select
   dimension:
~standard
Differences between STANDARD and current settings

STANDARD Current setting

DIMCLRT BYBLOCK  2 (Yellow)
DIMBLK1    _OBLIQUE
DIMBLK2    _OBLIQUE
DIMSAH Off    On
```

You can list any dimension's overrides with the list command as well.

To apply overrides to existing dimensions, you can also enter the old Dim prompt and execute the update command to update existing dimensions. This execution has the same effect as the Dimstyle/Apply option. A word of warning, however, the Dim prompt is doomed to disappear in future releases, so try to disassociate yourself from it as much as possible.

If you prefer the command prompt interface to setting overrides in the Ddim dialog box, there's a **dimoverride** command (dimove for short) you might also find handy:

```
Command: DIMOVERRIDE
Dimension variable to override (or Clear to remove
   overrides)
```

Input the dimension variable you want to change and the new value. The Clear option removes all existing overrides.

You'll then be asked to select any existing dimensions on which to put the overrides.

To return to the original Sample dimension style (no overrides), re-enter the **ddim** command and select Sample (without the +) from the dimension style listing. Many of these dimension commands are quite a handful to type (**dimoverride**). I would recommend aliasing these commands to eliminate any extra keystrokes (remember the ACAD.PGP file). If you're on the Windows build of AutoCAD Release 13 or Release 14, you could place the dimensioning toolbar on the screen as well.

As a general rule, temporary changes, such as suppressing a dimension line, should be handled with overrides; those more frequently used should be applied to a dimension style. Setting dimension style standards is an excellent way to control drafting standards in-house. Force yourself to create multiple dimension styles for the majority of your dimensioning needs, and save them in your prototype drawings. This process will eliminate the need to create these styles over and over again. A little preparation can save you countless hours of tedium. And let's face it, no matter how nice the Ddim dialog box looks, you don't want to spend any more time in it than absolutely necessary!

# Raise the Roof
# on Productivity

As new releases come and go, Autodesk typically improves upon existing commands and throws in a few new ones per the users' request. These modifications may be as simple as being able to explode a block where the *x* and *y* scale factors are not the same or being able to load the linetypes from within the layer dialog box Ddlmodes. While new users will find these modifications unexciting, veteran users of AutoCAD will find the changes to be great cause for celebration.

## Object Cycling

Have you ever tried to select one of two objects that are placed right on top of each other? With Release 11, AutoCAD always grabbed the last object drawn. Though simple, this process would often take longer than necessary because AutoCAD would search the entire database for an object. Release 12 modified this approach by introducing the concept of Oct-tree spatial indexing. Oct-tree spatial indexing breaks the current display into quadrants when searching for entities. This search method is faster and far superior to the traditional approach used in Release 11 and before. This newer method can, however, be frustrating when trying to locate one of several objects in close proximity to each other, which is where the new object cycling comes in.

Draw several lines that cross each other like an asterisk. Enter an editing command such as ERASE or MOVE and pick right at the intersection of these lines. Which line does it select? Oct-tree spatial indexing kicks in, splits the screen into quadrants and grabs one of the lines at random. Cancel and try again. This time we'll hold down <Control> while picking. Notice the words "cycle on" that display along the command prompt. Remove your finger from the control key and continue picking. AutoCAD will cycle through the objects one at a time. When the proper object is selected, hit <Enter> for the final selection. Object cycling may be used whenever the selected object's prompt is displayed. This tool is very handy yet simple.

## Groups

Another new method of object selection is the concept of groups. Similar to the block mindset comes this new ability to link objects together to form a group, which is a named group of objects that can be called on whenever needed. The members of these groups may be selected individually or as a team. We select unamed groups of objects via windows, fences, and so on all the time. Now we have the added capability of applying a name to these objects. Group definitions are stored within the drawing and follow externally referenced drawings as well.

Though there is a command line interface for the GROUP command (**-group**), we'll create our groups via a dialog box as shown in Figure 1. The GROUP command was designed with third-party developers in mind, but we'll find ways to use this feature to our advantage. Create a drawing with several circles and several rectangles. We'll use these objects to formulate our groups.

Under the Tools pull-down menu is an option called Object Group, which executes the GROUP command and takes us into

**Figure 1:** Object
Grouping dialog box.

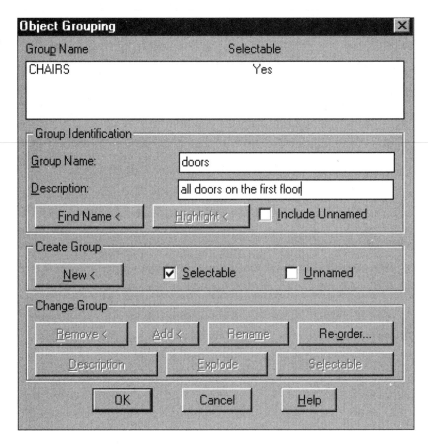

**Figure 1:** Object Grouping dialog box.

a dialog box. Begin by assigning a group name. Group names can be up to 31 characters in length and must follow all the assorted AutoCAD naming convention rules. Do yourself a favor and keep the group names short. You can add an optional description of your group if you desire (for future reference). Under the Create Group options, pick <New>. The dialog box will vanish, and you can select the objects you want included within the group using the usual object selection techniques.

Try creating a group called Cir that includes all your circles and a group called Box that includes all your rectangles. Both these groups will display in the Group dialog box. Both groups are selectable.

Enter an edit command (MOVE, COPY, ERASE, and so on) and when prompted to select objects, key in **g** (for group).

AutoCAD will ask you for the group name—enter **cir**. All the members of the Cir group will highlight.

```
Command: ERASE
Select objects: G
Enter Group name: CIR
```

You'll also notice that if you pick one of the members of a group, all the group members are selected. If you want to individually select the members of a group, you can do so by toggling Group mode off. This is done with a <Ctrl-A> (which can be entered anywhere). <Ctrl-A> toggles Group mode On or Off. Although Control-G seems like the logical choice for a Group combination key—remember that Control-G is already taken (Grid).

Let's review the other options within the Group dialog box. Under Group Identification, you'll see <Find Name>. This button removes the Group dialog box temporarily from the screen and lets you select an object. The group name display is convenient when you can't remember which group an object is a member of. Similar to this option is <Highlight>. When selected, AutoCAD will highlight the members of the group selected in the Group Name list box.

Should you copy a group, the resulting copied objects also belong to a group. The new group has a randomly generated name that doesn't display in the Group Name list box. To display this new group's name, select the Include Unnamed toggle.

There are two toggles under the Create Group section of the Object Grouping dialog box: Selectable and Unnamed. Similar to the previous comments, you can create a group with no name (actually it's a randomly generated name). This group doesn't display unless the Include Unnamed toggle is selected.

If a group is selectable, all of the objects within the group are treated as one group. When you select one member of the group—all are highlighted. An unselectable group doesn't have any group qualities at all. This option was generated with the

137

third-party applications in mind. Through LISP and ADS, groups could be selectable one minute and unselectable the next, which would keep any groups made by these external programs from getting in your way. I am unaware of any reason you'd be generating Unselectable groups.

After creating your groups, you may want to modify them. The Change Group section of the Object Grouping dialog box contains options to modify existing groups:

- Remove: deletes one or more objects from the current group.
- Add: adds one or more objects to the current group.
- Rename: changes the name of an existing group.
- Description: changes the group description.
- Explode: deletes an entire group (an important one to know).
- Selectable: changes the selectable status of an existing group.
- Re-order: changes the order of objects within an existing group.
  In some applications order is very important (tooling paths).

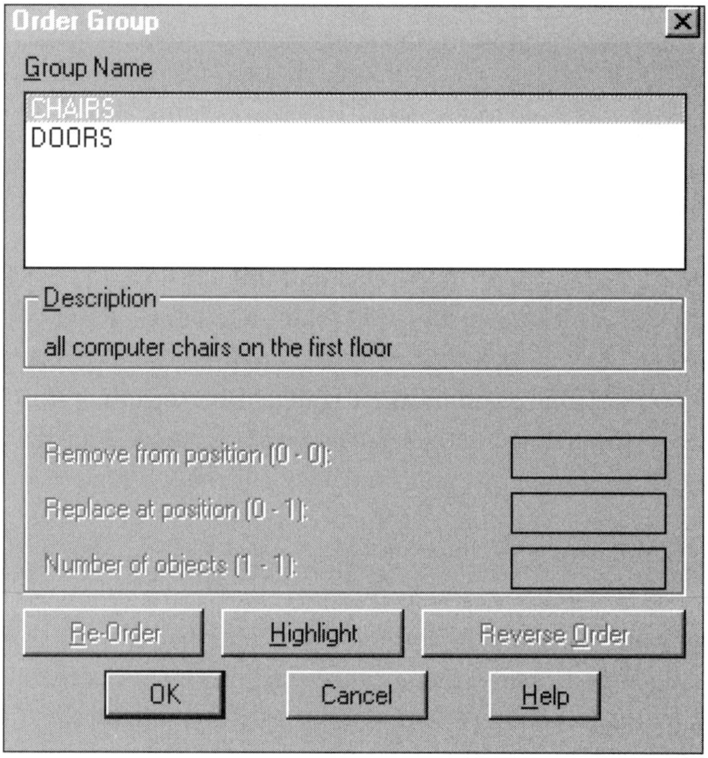

**Figure 2:** Order Group dialog box.

This last option takes you to a subdialog box as shown in Figure 2. This dialog box is only useful in very specific applications, so we won't spend much time on it. Essentially, you select the objects and assign those objects to a position.

What happens when an object is a member of more than one group? We'll create a group called Boxcir with one rectangle and one circle (be sure your group toggle is Off, or you'll never be able to select just one circle or rectangle).

Toggle Group mode back on <Ctrl-A> and enter an editing command. Select an object that is a member of two groups. Can you see how both groups are selected? If you would like to toggle between the two groups, use the object cycling we discussed previously. Select one of the members of the group while holding down the control key.

## LENGTHEN

There's another nice editing command called LENGTHEN. This command takes much of the guesswork out of simple length modifications. For example you want a line to be 5 inches long, it's currently 4 and ³⁄₈, how do you scale or stretch it quickly to the correct length? The LENGTHEN command is used to change the angle of arcs and the lengths of most open entities. Let's look at this command:

```
Command: LENGTHEN (MODIFY pull-down)
DELta/Percent/Total/DYnamic /<Select object>: pick an
   existing line
Current length: 5.4003
DELta/Percent/Total/DYnamic /<Select object>:T
Angle/<Enter total length (1.0000)>: 6
<Select object to change>/ Undo:
Let's review the options:
```

- Select object: provides the current length/included angle of a selected object.
- Delta: increases or decreases the selected objects by a specified increment. When dealing with arcs, you may suggest a

delta angle. Positive values increase the length of selected objects, Negative values decrease the length. The object is lengthened/shortened from the endpoint nearest the pick point on the object. If you specified a delta angle of 45 degrees, any arc selected would increase in size by an arc of 45 degrees.

- Percent: uses a specified percentage of an object's total length to increase or decrease the selected objects. If you specified a total percentage of 50 percent, the length of the selected objects would be cut in half.
- Total: you select the total length you'd like an object to have, and AutoCAD calculates for you, which might entail trimming or extending the object to get the desired results. Any modifications occur from the nearest endpoint.
- Dynamic: visually changes the length of an object by moving the nearest endpoint.

The key to the LENGTHEN command is ensuring, that you pick the objects to lengthen towards the end you want to affect. All new commands take a while to filter into your daily work practices—be sure to force yourself to try them out.

We've covered just a few of the many productivity enhancements introduced in AutoCAD Release 13. Taking advantage of these underexposed features should shorten drawing time and add some variety to your AutoCAD world.

# Misc. Productivity Enhancements

This chapter contains a few of the neglected yet cool features that reside in AutoCAD. You'll already know about some of them—but I hope you'll find at least one or two you can tuck away and use on a rainy CAD day.

## Change Point Option in the CHANGE Command

The CHANGE command has long been replaced with the more efficient dialog boxes Ddmodify and Ddchprop. R13 went one step further by placing these dialog boxes within the Properties button on the Object Property toolbar. The age-old CHANGE command still has a unique option not found anywhere else called Change Point. Suppose you have five parallel lines that you want to extend to a specific point, as shown in Figure 1. The CHANGE command can extend these lines in one quick step. The EXTEND command couldn't do that nearly as efficiently.

```
Command: CHANGE
Select objects: select the objects you want to change
Select objects:
Properties/<Change point>: select the point you want the
   lines to extend to
```

**Figure 1:** Parallel
lines to be extended.

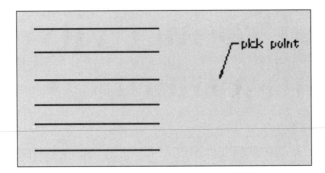

**Figure 2:** Change
Point with Ortho ON

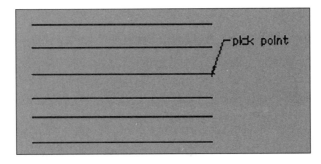

**Figure 3:** Change
Point with Ortho OFF

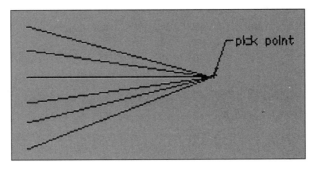

You will get very different results, depending on your Ortho
mode, as shown in Figures 2 and 3.

## Presetting Scale Factors and Rotation Angles in the INSERT Command

I've often felt that the INSERT and DDINSERT commands are
structured backwards. I wish I could scale or rotate my symbol
before I show AutoCAD where I want to place it. As it stands
now, I select my insertion point first only to realize that, after
rotating and scaling it, my object has been inserted at a poor

location. Consequently, I end up moving my object after the fact, an extra step I find very frustrating. If you can relate, you'll appreciate the next tip.

There are secret options hidden within the INSERT command (we wouldn't want everyone to find out and become too productive!). When prompted for the Insertion Point, AutoCAD will accept a total of 10 options that relate to scaling and rotating. Whichever programmer snuck this stuff into AutoCAD should be commended (if only that person had a good PR agent to promote this hidden feature). Let's say you would like to rotate your object 90 degrees before selecting an insertion point:

```
Command:INSERT (or DDINSERT)
Block name (or ?): widget
Insertion point: R (for rotate)
Rotation angle: 90
Insertion point: X scale factor <1> / Corner / XYZ:
Y scale factor (default=X):
```

Notice that AutoCAD doesn't reprompt you for the rotation angle because you've already answered that question. Other options accepted at the Insertion Point prompt include:

```
S: Scale factor (X and Y)
X: X scale factor
Y: Y scale factor
Z: Z scale factor
```

If you'd like to preselect a rotation angle or scale factor and have AutoCAD prompt you for this value again after selection, you can use the following options:

```
PS: Preselect Scale factor
PX: Preselect X scale factor
PY: Preselect Y scale factor
PZ: Preselect Z scale factor
PR: Preselect Rotation angle
```

I never use the preselect options. I don't care for the redundancy.

## Automatic Dimensioning

I am still amazed at the number of AutoCAD operators who work much harder than necessary when it comes to dimensioning. Do you always manually select the two endpoints of extension lines? If so, you're working too hard. When dimensioning to the endpoints of lines, AutoCAD can do the job much faster than you can, so put it to work! Let's use the DIMLINEAR command as an example:

```
Command: DIMLINEAR
First extension line origin or hit Enter to select: (hit
  enter)
Select object to dimension:
```

After hitting [Enter], a pickbox appears and you simply select the part you want to dimension. AutoCAD will find the two endpoints of the object selected for you—no object snaps are required!

## Creating Hatch Patterns Without a Boundary (R13 and R14 Only)

R12 introduced the powerful BHATCH command. I think it's safe to say that, at that point, most of us turned our backs on the age-old standard HATCH command. Just when we thought the HATCH command would become a thing of the past, R13 added a clever feature to it. The standard HATCH command allows you to create a hatch pattern without a boundary. In essence, you create this polyline boundary on the fly, and you can choose to keep it or discard it. If you ever want to stick a hatch pattern into your drawing quickly but don't want a boundary in the finished product, try this clever trick.

```
Command: HATCH
Pattern (? or name/U,style) <ANSI31>: BRICK (key in the
  name of the pattern)
Scale for pattern <1.0000>:
Angle for pattern <0>:
```

```
Select hatch boundaries or RETURN for direct hatch option,
Select objects: enter
Retain polyline? <N>
From point:
Arc/Close/Length/Undo/<Next point>:
Arc/Close/Length/Undo/<Next point>:
Arc/Close/Length/Undo/<Next point>:
Arc/Close/Length/Undo/<Next point>:
From point or RETURN to apply hatch: enter
```

The latter part of this command is used to create a temporary polyline that AutoCAD can use as a boundary.

## The Displacement Option in the COPY and MOVE Commands

If you want to move an object in your drawing over three units to the right, how would you do it? Chances are very good that you'd use the MOVE command, and chances are even better that you'd take an extra step more than is necessary to do it. Have you ever taken advantage of the Displacement option in the COPY and MOVE commands? After all, Displacement is the default. Most of you would move an object over three units using the following method:

```
Command: MOVE
Select objects: 1 found
Select objects:
Base point or displacement: pick a base point
Second point of displacement:@3,0
```

Well, I'd say you're taking an extra unnecessary step (plus that @ symbol is a pain) Try this option:

```
Command: MOVE
Select objects: 1 found
Select objects:
Base point or displacement: 3,0
Second point of displacement: (enter)
```

Notice the prompt reads Base point or displacement. Displacement is the actual default, but we all seem to select a base point. Perhaps if the command read Base point or <displacement>, it would be more obvious. The trick is to hit an extra [Enter] when prompted for a second point, which tells AutoCAD to use that 3,0 (3 over on the *x* axis, 0 on the *y* axis) as a displacement value.

## Object Selection Techniques

What if you wanted to select all of the objects in a particular area except for one? Would you create a couple of windows and avoid that one object? Would you pick all of the objects individually? Or would you select all of the objects quickly and easily with a window and remove the one object you don't want to include? I vote for the last method. We used to remove objects by using the R notation to jump into the Remove Objects mode. Now, it's a piece of cake with the [Shift] key. Holding down the [Shift] key while selecting objects will remove objects from the selection set.

## Concealing Viewports in Paper Space

I'd be lying if I told you I dreamed this one up myself. One of my readers sent this great suggestion to me. While in Paper Space, we want to see our viewports while we're creating and editing our drawing but not when we print. Consequently, we put viewports into our drawing on their own layer and freeze that layer when it's time to plot our drawing. Why not break AutoCAD etiquette and put the viewports on the Defpoints layer? The Defpoints layer is unique in that we can see the objects placed on this layer, yet they never plot. This is perfect for viewports (and assorted construction objects). Just be careful not to put any other objects on that layer—you'll think you're in the twilight zone when they don't show up in the final output.

## Intersecting with Appint

Appint stands for Apparent Intersection. This object snap was
sent from the 3D gods to help us grab visual intersections.
Imagine you're looking at your drawing from a viewing angle
where two entities look as though they cross, but in 3D reality,
they don't. With Release 12, you could never grab the two entities' "apparent intersection." If those two entities didn't really
cross, you were out of luck. With Release 13 and 14, if two entities appear to intersect in your current viewing plane—appint
will find a way to grab this intersection.

Unlike the object snap modes in the past, appint also permits
picking two entities rather than one. Let's say you wanted to
draw a line from the intersection where two entities apparently
intersect. The two entities below were drawn on two different
ucs's. We can see a visual intersection from this viewing angle,
although they don't physically intersect in space. When
prompted for a start point of your line:

```
Command: LINE
From point: APPINT
of pick1 (pick the visual intersection)
```

You could also have AutoCAD find the apparent intersection
by picking the entities one at a time:

```
Command: LINE
From point: APPINT
of pick1 (pick one of the entities)
pick2 (pick the other entity)
```

The final pickpoint is determined by the following very
important rules:

- The point returned lies on the apparent intersection of the
  first entity selected.
- If more than one apparent intersection is possible, AutoCAD
  will pick the intersection closest to the two selection points.
- When picking two entities simultaneously, the point will lie

on the last entity drawn. Selecting the entities individually permits you to have more control over the final pickpoint.

The intersection object snap became more intelligent in Release 13, as well. Let's go back to 2D thinking. Have you ever wished AutoCAD was smart enough to mentally extend two entities until they meet and grab this imagined intersection? You don't want these two entities physically extended, but you do want the point of intended intersection. Welcome to the new intersection object snap. From now on, we'll refer to this as an extended intersection.

**Figure 4:** Extended intersection.

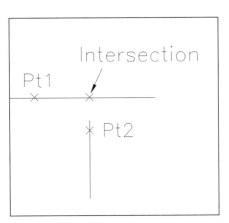

Take a look at Figure 4. You pick Point 1 and Point 2. AutoCAD will return the extended intersection Point 3. Note that this option will not work on the new splines.

## The From Object Snap

The From object snap will save you countless tedious construction steps. Do you use the id command frequently to record a lastpoint value? How would you create the following circle one inch over and one inch up from the lower left hand corner of the box? Would you draw a construction mark and change your ucs? The new from object snap fits nicely into such predicaments. From will prompt you for a base point (reference point) and an offset, and can also be paired with other object snaps:

```
Command: CIRCLE
2P/3P/TTR<Center point>: FROM
Base point: (pick the lower left-hand corner of the box)
<Offset>: @ 1,1
```

The offset could also have been expressed in polar coordination notation (dist<angle). My only complaint about this option is the need to input the "@" symbol. If it's asking me for an offset, doesn't that assume relative? The correct AutoCAD answer is no.

## Fillet and Chamfer

Fillet and chamfer have also been updated and enhanced. In past releases, these commands were not forgiving if you were a bad shot during the selection process. If you accidentally missed one of the intended entities, AutoCAD shot you right out of the command. Release 13 and 14 will give you another try. In fact, you can have as many tries as you might need. But that enhancement isn't the only one.

How many times have you had to check the current radius value (distances for chamfer)? AutoCAD has never displayed the default value. From this point, on the default value will be displayed prominently at the beginning of the command.

In the past, fillet and chamfer would often trim off portions of open entities which were not included in the final fillet or chamfer. If you filleted between two items, the final outcome would quite often result in the removal of a line segment. We would often redraw these segments back in after the fact. Release 13 provides the means to trim or not to trim:

```
Command: Fillet
(Trim mode) Current fillet radius = 0.75
Polyline/Radius/Trim/<Select first object>: trim
Trim/No Trim: No
Polyline/Radius/Trim/<Select first object>: (Pick an
   entity)
Select second object: Pick an entity
```

This operation will leave the entities selected intact. For those of you who prefer system variables, you can also use the new system variable trimmode to achieve the same effect. When trimmode is set to 1, the fillet and chamfer commands will trim back the selected entities when necessary. When trimmode is set to 0, AutoCAD will not trim the selected entities back.

Have you ever tried to fillet or chamfer between a line and a polyline? It won't happen in Release 12 or before. Release 13 lightened up the polyline restrictions. You can now painlessly fillet or chamfer between a line and a polylines. The fillet (or chamfer) will join the two into one polyline. If notrim is on, a fillet arc will be added to the drawing and the entities will remain as they were originally.

The new updated fillet will also cap off two parallel lines with a fillet arc as seen in Figure 5. You don't indicate a fillet radius— it is calculated for you. The diameter of the fillet arc will be equal to the distance between the two parallel lines. The fillet arc will begin at the nearest endpoint of the entity selected first.

The chamfers in AutoCAD have always been calculated by using two distances. You have provided the input distance you wanted each leg to be cut back by. The real drafting world has calculated chamfers with angles. Release 13 finally accomodated this technique. A new Method option allows you to select either distance-distance or a length-angle combination.

**Figure 5:** Filleting parallel lines.

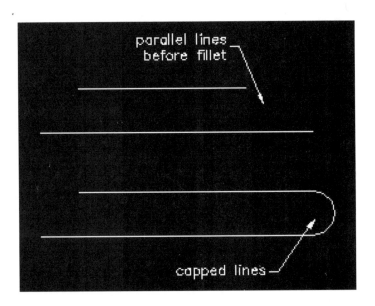

```
Command: CHAMFER
(TRIM mode)Current chamfer Dist1 = 0.25, Dist2 = 0.25
Polyline/Distances/Angle/Trim/Method/<Select first line>:
  Angle
Enter chamfer length on first line: 0.5
Enter chamfer angle from the first line <0.000> 30
Polyline/Distances/Angle/Trim/Method/<Select first line>:
  pick
Select second line: pick again
Linetype Scales
```

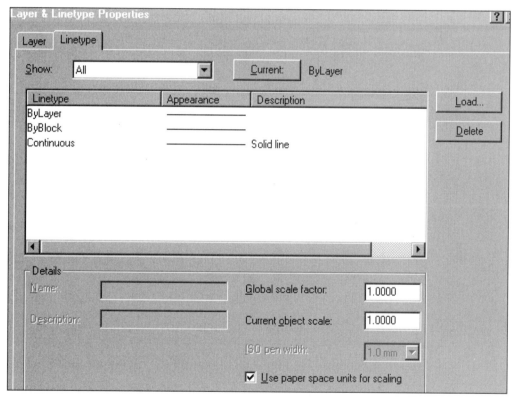

**Figure 6:** Line type dialog box.

One more small yet important feature is linetype scales. No doubt also on the wishlist for years has been the need for multiple linetype scales per drawing. We've always had the all-encompassing ltscale command. Inserting a drawing with linetypes into another drawing with differing ltscale settings could prove disastrous. Now you can attribute a linetype scale setting to one or more individual entities. The entities carry this setting with them. This new ability has been incorporated into the commands we are already familiar with: chprop, ddchprop, and ddmodify. The CELTSCALE command can be used to set a Current Entity Linetype scale factor as well. This can be found in the Details section of the Linetype tab in the Layer dialog box as shown in Figure 6.

It isn't always the major new features of a software product that make it more valuable. Fine-tuning the existing product can be just as valuable (and often more so, especially to the experienced AutoCAD user.

# The Finale: Taking the Reins of AutoCAD

# Lost in Paper Space

Paper Space is a simple concept, yet quite difficult to explain effectively (especially on paper). I have seen instructors go to great lengths creating visual aids just to get this idea into the heads of their students. Once the lightbulb goes off and you comprehend this logical world, you'll wonder how you survived without it. But until then, you may find that Paper Space (and Model Space) is frustrating and not user friendly. This month, I'll make a noble attempt to change your views on this very important topic and show you just how simple it is. Because there has been little change to Paper Space in Release 13, those of you using previous releases should feel right at home.

Who needs Paper Space? Anyone who creates drawings containing multiple scale factors. Anyone who creates 3D drawings and wants to plot multiple views. Anyone who wants to draw one-to-one and plot one-to-one. Anyone who is tired of multiplying text and dimensions to outrageous sizes so they're scaled correctly for models. Anyone who wants to clip External References (perhaps for Details) and combine any number of them per sheet.

Chances are, you fall into one of these categories. Let's start at the very beginning.

**1.** You open a new drawing. Now, you are living in the world of Model Space. How do you know? The UCSICON in the lower-left-hand corner of the drawing editor looks like Figure 1 and the system variable **tilemode** is set to 1. If you are using Release 13, you'll notice that the words MODEL and TILE are selected. To absolutely verify that you're in Model Space, you can key in the word **tilemode** at the command prompt at any time. A value of 1 indicates you're in the Model World; a value of 0 indicates you're in the Paper World.

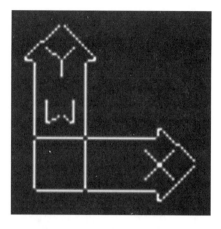

**Figure 1:** The UCSICON in the Model Space world.

If you typically work with the UCSICON set to 0, you'll need to turn it back on to survive in the Paper and Model Space worlds. If you don't, it will be very difficult for you to determine where you are at any given time, as shown in Figure 1.

Now what exactly does **tilemode** have to do with anything? Excellent question! **Tilemode** controls whether your viewports are tiled or not. When you're in Model Space, you can only create viewports that are tiled as shown in Figure 2. Tiled viewports mean they must lie edge to edge (**tilemode** is on). Tiled

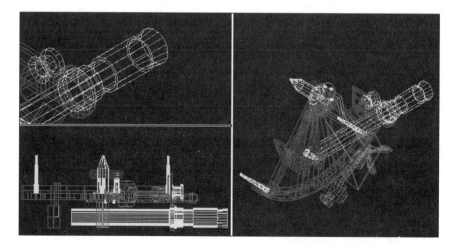

**Figure 2:** When you're in Model Space, you can only create viewports that are tiled.

155

viewports are created using the VPORTS command (and have been around for quite a while). They are used to show several different views of your drawing simultaneously. You cannot, however, plot more than one view at a time. The PLOT command only plots the active view. Viewports in the Model World are basically used only for display purposes. When **tilemode** is set to 1, you cannot click on the Paper Space button on the status line.

When you're in Paper Space, there are no viewport rules. Viewports can overlap, lie one within the other, and so on. They do not have to be tiled (hence **tilemode** is off). Viewports can be copied, moved, stretched, erased, and so on. Viewports take on very different properties when in Paper Space. You can actually plot more than one viewport when you're in the Paper World.

**2.** So, you're in your new drawing, and you are in Model Space. **Tilemode** is set to 1. Now, you create your model, 2D or 3D, at a scale factor of one-to-one. If you're drawing a house that's 50 x 40 feet, you'll draw it exactly that size. If you're drawing a sensor that's 4mm x 2mm, then draw it exactly that size. Set up your drawing limits, snap, and grid accordingly. So far you're not doing anything different than you've done in the past. Create only the model; we'll add title blocks, text, and dimensions later.

**3.** You've created your model, and now it's time to annotate your drawing. Now, we'll take that jump into the Paper World. By now, you should know exactly how we're going to get there!

If you're using Release 13, hit the Tile button on the Status bar. This action will automatically set **tilemode** to 0 (turn **tilemode** off). If you're using Release 12, you can manually key in **tilemode** or use the View pull-down menu to find the Tilemode option. If you're using AutoCAD for Windows (R12 or R13), you should see that the Paper Space button on the Tile Bar is selected. Regardless of platform, the UCSICON in the lower left hand corner of the drawing editor should now look like Figure 3.

So where's your model? It's in the Model World where it belongs. Anything you create in the Model World stays in the

Model World and anything created in the Paper World remains in the Paper World. We'll get your model in a minute.

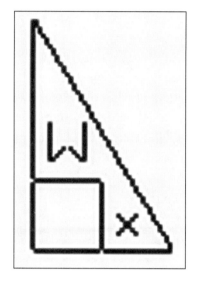

**4.** Congratulations, you've made it to the Paper World. You should be looking at an empty drawing again; the limits are more than likely set to 9 x 12 units with the grid 1 unit apart. The Paper World needs to be set up to emulate the hard copy with which you're going to end up. If you plan on outputting to a B-Size sheet of paper, set your units to 16 x 10. For those of you living in metric, if you wanted an A3 sheet of paper, you'd set the limits to 396 x 273mm. Set up your limits to equal the size of the paper you plan on using to plot. You might want to set your snap and grid accordingly.

Do you have a title block you'd like to use? Insert it now to fit on your paper the way you want it to plot. Fill in the title block with the appropriate text information.

**5.** Now, you have your paper all set up and ready to go. All you need now is your model. We'll go get our model and bring it into the Paper World via the MVIEW command. There's quite a difference of opinion about what the M in MVIEW stands for. I've heard Model View, Make View, and Meta View—you can take your pick.

It's also very important to bring your model in on its own layer. I suggest creating a layer called MVIEW or VIEWPORT (whatever works for you) expressly for this purpose. When you bring your model in, you'll notice a nice rectangular boundary comes with it. Before you plot, you'll probably want to suppress that boundary, which can be done by turning the VIEWPORT layer off.

157

So you've created a new layer and made it current, now you're ready to get your model. MVIEW is located in the View pull-down menu (View=>Floating Model Space) in Release 13 or in the View=>Mview pull-down in Release 12. Using the MVIEW command, pick two opposite corners on the paper where you'd like the model to be placed. This option is the default in the MVIEW command. Feel free to reenter the command and create a couple more views of your model just for practice. This step is refered to as opening windows to the Model World.

Notice how they can overlap, and even be placed within each other, as shown in Figure 4.

You can create as many viewports as you want, but by default only 16 viewports will display at any given time. You can turn individual viewports on and off to control which viewports display and which do not.

These viewports are objects, which means they can be moved, copied, stretched, and so on. They even have grips. Try editing these viewports so you're comfortable with these new objects.

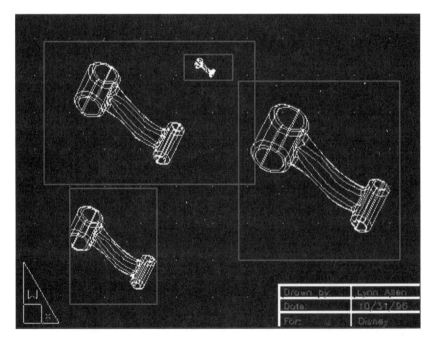

**Figure 4:** You can create as many viewports as you want, but only 15 viewports will display at any given time.

Let's review the other options in the MVIEW command:

```
Command: mview
ON/OFF/Hideplot/Fit/2/3/4/Restore/<First Point>:
```

**First Point:** The default option requires that the user select two points to define the viewport.

**ON:** Turns the selected viewports ON, making their contents visible.

**OFF:** Turns the selected viewports OFF, making their contents invisible. If a viewport is off, you cannot make that viewport current.

**Hideplot:** By default, AutoCAD will not hide the models within the viewports when plotting. This option allows you to select those viewports you want AutoCAD to issue the HIDE command on for plotting purposes.

**Fit:** Creates one viewport that fills the entire display area.

**2:** Creates two equal viewports, side by side. You will be asked to specify horizontal or vertical. Also select the area in which you want these two viewports to reside (by selecting the two opposite corners) or use the **Fit** option to fill the entire display with these two viewports.

**3:** Divides the selected area into three viewports: one large viewport and two smaller viewports (similar to the VPORTS command). You must decide if you want the large viewport placed above, below, to the right, or to the left of the two smaller viewports.

**4:** Divides the selected area into four tiled viewports of equal size. You can select the area in which you want these four viewports to go or use the **Fit** option to fill the entire display.

**RESTORE:** This option is interesting. If you created tiled viewports while in the Model World and saved the configuration, you can bring that same configuration into Paper Space by using the Restore option of the MVIEW command. You will be prompted for the name of the saved viewport configuration and where you'd like them to go. The model will come in exactly as they were last displayed in that saved viewport configuration.

**6.** You can go inside any of these model views by entering the command MS (Model Space) at the command prompt. This step can also be done by deselecting the Paper button on the status line. You'll notice that all of the viewports have their own UCSICON in the lower-left-hand corner of the view. Your cross-hairs are lying within one of these viewports—this is the active viewport. You can pan, zoom, and edit your model from within this viewport. You can also move from viewport to viewport by clicking inside the viewport you want to be active.

If you were overzealous and created a viewport completely within another viewport, you may have also noticed that once you select the larger viewport, you can no longer get into the smaller viewport. No problem. <Ctrl+V> allows you to bounce from one viewport to another without picking any-thing on the screen. Try using <Ctrl+V> to cycle through all of the viewports.

Now, take a deep breath and think about what's going on. You're in Model Space, while you're in the Paper World. You can actually make modifications to your model right here. If you go back to the Model World (**tilemode** set to 1), will these changes affect your original Model? You bet! There is only one model, and you're always working on the original. Then it stands to reason that if you reset **tilemode** to 1 and return to the model and make changes to the model in the Model World, that when you return to the Paper World (**tile-mode** =0) the modifications will be reflected here as well. That's also a correct assumption. It doesn't matter where you make changes to the model—you're modifying the one and only model.

While in the Paper World, you can bounce in and out of your viewports by keying in **MS** or **PS**. **MS** puts you inside of a viewport, **PS** takes you to your overall paper layout. You can also use the Paperspace button on the status line.

## Let's step through the process so far:

**1.** You are in Model Space—because tilemode is set to 1. Create your model at a 1:1 scale. Do not place any dimensions or text on your drawing.

**2.** Now, you're ready to enter the Paper World by setting tilemode to 0. You can also enter the Paper World by double clicking on the Tile button on the Status bar (Release 13 and14 only). You will know you're in the Paper World because the UCSICON in the lower-left-hand corner of your drawing screen now resembles a triangle. Set your limits to equal the size of the paper you'll be plotting on. Insert a title block if desired.

**3.** Create a viewport layer and make it current. Now, we'll go get the model and place it on the paper. This process is done with the MVIEW command. Pick the two opposite corners of a window you'd like your model to fit into on your paper. Put a couple of viewports of your model in your drawing, so we have something to work with.

Should you choose to work within the viewports on your model (while in the Paper World), you can key in MS (for Model Space). You can also click on the Paper Space button on the status line (Windows R12 or R13 only). This action will not change the value of tilemode, but it will make one of the viewports active (or current). You can move from viewport to viewport by picking within the desired viewport. You can also use <Ctrl+V> to change the active viewport. Notice that, as you Pan and Zoom, you're just modifying the display within the active viewport. If you key in PS to return to Paper Space and Zoom, you'll see you're zooming relative to the entire sheet of paper.

Golden rule: Those things you create in Paper space can only be edited within Paper Space. Those things you create in Model Space can only be edited within Model Space.

Now, we're ready to dive deeper into the world of Paper Space. You should have at least two viewports of your model on your screen. Make one of the viewports active by keying in MS (or clicking on the status line).

## Scale Factors

What scale factor are our models using? We created them at 1:1, full scale, but who knows what they are set to now? We must be able to control the scale factors of these models with the viewports, which is done by using the XP option within the trusty ZOOM command—not exactly a logical assumption. XP stands for "Times Paper Space." The next part gets a little confusing.

What would you like your scale factor to be within this viewport? One-quarter inch equals one foot? Or did you create something really small that you'd like to make larger with a scale factor of 2:1? Let's start with the simple architectural scale factor of $1/4"=1'$.

If you were drafting on a piece of paper, the scale factor of $1/4"=1'$ would mean that you were scaling everything down to fit on your paper. In fact, you'd be dividing all the real world measurements by 48. Where did I get 48? Simple: $1/4=12$ is the ratio. So take 4, multiply it by 12, and you get 48; you end up with $1/48$. $1/2"=1'$ gives you $1/24$, $1"=1'$ gives you $1/12$, and so on.

To scale objects up: 2:1 is equal to 1 divided by 2 yielding .5, 4:1 is equal to 1 divided by 4 yielding .25, and so on.

| Table 1. Scale factors | |
|---|---|
| ½ inch = 1 foot | ZOOM ¹⁄₂₄XP |
| ⅜ inch = 1 foot | ZOOM ¹⁄₃₂XP |
| ¼ inch = 1 foot | ZOOM ¹⁄₄₈XP |
| ⅛ inch = 1 foot | ZOOM ¹⁄₉₆XP |
| 2 = 1 | ZOOM 2XP |
| 4 = 1 | ZOOM 4XP |

If you want the scale factor within one of your viewports to be $1/4"=1'$, enter the ZOOM command within the desired viewport and then enter $1/48$XP. This command will divide your full-scale model by 48 within the viewport. You can easily make another viewport active and set the scale factor to something different by entering the ZOOM command and setting a different XP value. After setting the appropriate ZOOM scale factor, use the PAN command in the viewport to position the model properly within the viewport. See how easy it is to have multiple scale factors per drawing when you use Paper Space? A chart for some basic scale factors is shown in Table 1.

Remember, we're just taking the full-scale model and scaling it down to fit on the paper.

## Dimensioning

So, you've set up your viewports to the proper scale factor. Now, how do we go about dimensioning our model? Should we do it in Paper Space or Model Space? We'll be in the Paper World (tilemode is off), but we'll dimension within the floating viewports (Model Space).

While in Paper Space, Zoom up on the viewport you will be dimensioning. Switch over to Model Space, and make it the active viewport. Create and set a layer specifically for the dimensions you will be placing within this viewport. To ensure that we get properly scaled dimensions, we'll select the Scale to Paper Space option within the DDIM dialog box (Release 13 and 14). If you're in Release 12, select Use Paper Space Scaling within any of the dialog boxes accessed by DDIM. Behind the scenes, we're actually setting the dimension variable dimscale to 0. Set all the other dimension variables to the actual settings you want the dimensions to have (WYSIWYG). If you want the text to be ⅜-inch high, you should set the dimension text to that height.

Here's the tricky part: when you dimension, AutoCAD will look at the scale factor set within the viewport and use that value to calculate the outcome of the size of the final dimension. It does this calculation automatically, to ensure that you get the text, dimension lines, extension lines, and so on exactly the size you want without any extra hassle. AutoCAD does all the calculations for you. You only need to set this up once and it works for all viewports.

Should you choose to dimension another viewport, you simply switch to another viewport, create and set another layer for these new dimensions, and dimension away. AutoCAD will reevaluate the scale factor for this new viewport.

You may have noticed that the dimensions from the first viewport are showing up in the second viewport. This situation may not be desirable, which brings us to the next topic: the ability to control layer visibility from viewport to viewport.

## Viewport Layer Control

One of the most impressive benefits of using Paper Space is the ability to control layer visibility per viewport. For example, you might have the DIM1 layer visible in one viewport but not in another. This feature is very important to the success of Paper Space. You can't do that with the standard tiled viewports of the Model World.

Paper Space has its very own LAYER command called VPLAYER (ViewPort Layer). VPLAYER allows you to freeze or thaw individual layers per viewport. We'll start off with this command-prompt driven command and then migrate to DDLMODES, the Layer dialog box.

You must have tilemode set to 0 to enter the VPLAYER command. If a layer is already universally frozen (LAYER command), you cannot use VPLAYER to affect its visibility. The standard LAYER command always wins. If you are in Model Space when you execute this command, VPLAYER will automatically switch to Paper Space when needed. When the command is completed, you will be returned to Model Space. The VPLAYER command permits the use of wildcards as well (* and ?). It's often faster to enter the VPLAYER command and use wildcards than it is to manually select a group of layers in the layer dialog box. You'll see many Paper Spacers using this command on a regular basis, even though it's command-prompt driven because of its extra capabilities.

```
Command: vplayer
?/Freeze/Thaw/Reset/Newfrz/Vpvisdflt:
```

- The **?** option provides a list of the frozen layers in the selected viewport.
- The **Freeze** option is used to specify the layers you want to freeze. The following three suboptions will appear when you use Freeze: All freezes the specified layer(s) in all viewports, Select freezes the specified layer(s) in the viewports you select, and Current freezes the specified layer(s) in the current viewport only.
- The **Thaw** option thaws the specified layers in the selected viewports. When you use Thaw, the same three suboptions listed for Freeze will display.
- The Reset option resets the layers back to the default frozen or thawed state (see VPVISDFLT). You can reset the layers in the Current viewport, All the viewports, or Selected viewports.
- The **Newfrz** (New Freeze) option is used to create new layers that are frozen in all viewports. Why would you want to do that? When you have multiple floating viewports in your drawing, you often need to create a new layer that is visible in only one viewport. Use the Newfrz option to create this new layer, which will be frozen in all the viewports. Then, go to the desired viewport and thaw that new layer. This process is much easier than creating the layer and then freezing it in all of the other viewports. I know it seems like a roundabout way of achieving something, but it works!
- The **VPVISDFLT (Viewport Visibility Default)** option is the last. If this option doesn't intimidate you, nothing in AutoCAD will! Before explaining this option, let me set up an appropriate scenario (because I'm sure your head is swimming by now).

Paper Space is an ideal method of creating detail sheets. Let's say you have many different drawings that contain your details. You just want to get those details and bring them all together into one final sheet. Start a new drawing, and go immediately to Paper Space. Set up your paper (tilemode is off) and create your first MVIEW. The first detail will go here. Enter the viewport (MS), execute the XREF command, and attach the first detail drawing.

If you create another viewport for your next detail, you'll see that your first detail inconveniently displays in your second viewport as well. What to do? You could enter the VPLAYER command and use the Freeze option to freeze all the layers in the new viewport. But you would end up freezing layers in all subsequent viewports as well. The VPVISDFLT option comes into play at this point. Before creating your second viewport, you can tell AutoCAD that you want to freeze all those layers from the first detail in all new viewports. Because external references assign the drawing name as a prefix to the layer names, it is easy to use wildcards to control this layer visibility.

You can use VPVISDFLT to Freeze or Thaw layers in new viewports. If you accidentally put the cart before the horse by creating the viewport first and then realizing you need to change the VPVISDFLT, it's not a problem. You can use the Reset option to update any existing viewports.

Have I lost you yet? As I mentioned before, Paper Space is a difficult concept to comprehend. But when the lightbulb goes on, you'll realize how simple and logical Paper Space actually is. You'll wonder how you survived without it, and you'll insist on showing your newfound expertise to your coworkers.

Let's look at DDLMODES. Though somewhat more limited than VPLAYER, you might find this visual control easier than VPLAYER. Before entering DDLMODES, be sure to enter Model Space and set your current viewport to the one you want to modify. DDLMODES only affects the current viewport, as shown in Figure 5.

### Release 12-13: CurVP

Located on the right-hand side of the Layer dialog box, CurVP controls the visibility of layers within the current viewport. Thw will thaw the highlighted layers, Frz will freeze them. When a layer is frozen in the current viewport, a C appears next to the selected layer in the Layer dialog box. After

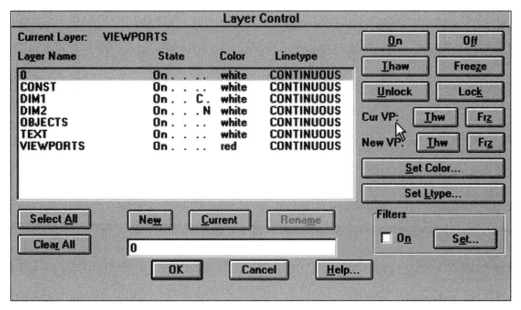

**Figure 5:** The Layer Control dialog box.

hitting the final OK, AutoCAD will regenerate all the viewports and update the drawing to reflect the changes.

### Release 12-13:  NewVP

Also located on the right-hand side of the Layer dialog box, NewVP controls the visibility of layers in all new viewports. When selected, an N will appear next to the selected layer. This option is similar to the Vpvisdflt option in VPLAYER.

### Release 14:  Freeze in Current Viewport

Freeze in Current Viewport controls the visibility of layers within the current viewport. Changing the icon to a sun will thaw the highlighted layers, changing the icon to a snowflake will freeze them. After hitting the final OK, AutoCAD will regenerate all the viewports and update the drawing to reflect the changes.

### Release 14:  Freeze in New Viewport

Freeze in New Viewport controls the visibility of layers in all newly created viewports. When selected, a snowflake will appear next to the selected layer. This option is similar to the Vpvisdflt option in VPLAYER.

167

## Miscellaneous Notes

If you have multiple floating viewports within Paper Space, regenerations can get painful because AutoCAD insists on regenerating every single viewport. If you don't need to use a viewport for awhile, by all means, turn the viewport off (MVIEW command). Though AutoCAD can display an unlimited number of viewports, your operating system determines the number of viewports that can be active at any given time. The MAXACTVP system variable internally controls the maximum number of active viewports AutoCAD will enable at any given time. The default value is 16, but a lower setting could improve your performance because inactive viewports are not regenerated.

If you plan to use xrefs in Paper Space, be sure to turn visretain to 1. This setting will ensure that your Layer settings (which you've so carefully set up) are saved with your drawing. this can be easily done using the details section in the AutoCAD Release 14 Layer dialog box.

When you plot multiple viewports, by default, AutoCAD will not remove hidden lines. To remove hidden lines within viewports, you will need to use the MVIEW command (Hideplot option) to select the desired viewports.

Also important is the psltscale variable. When set to a value of 1, AutoCAD uses the scale factor within the viewport to control the linetype scaling. This setting permits different magnifications while displaying identical linetypes.

So, now that you've set up your viewports, you might want the box to disappear around the edges of the viewport. Make sure you are in Paper Space, then freeze the layer on which you've placed the viewports. You'll find yourself with a finished drawing with multiple scale factors and views. When you create your final plot, the scale factor is 1:1. It couldn't be easier.

Now, let me step through the entire process one last time.

## The 10 Steps of Paper Space

1. Tilemode is set to 1. You are in the Model World. Create your model at a 1:1 scale factor.

2. Go to the Paper world. Tilemode is set to 0. Set up your limits, units, grid, snap, and so on for the actual paper to which you plan on plotting. Insert a border if desired.

3. Create and set a layer for your viewports. Be sure to use this layer for viewports only because you'll be freezing this layer when you make your final plot.

4. Use the MVIEW command to bring in your model.

5. Enter MS, and scale your model using the ZOOM XP option. Pan your drawing around if necessary to position it properly within the viewport.

6. Dimension the model. Be sure to set the dimensioning scale factor to Scale to Paper Space (or set dimscale to 0). If you have multiple viewports, use a different dimensioning layer for each viewport.

7. While in Paper Space, annotate your drawing. Set the text height to the actual size you want the final text to plot.

8. Use the MVIEW command to select any viewports in which you want AutoCAD to perform a hidden line removal (3D users only).

9. Freeze the viewport layer.

10. Plot at a scale factor of 1:1.

Though this overview of Paper Space is fairly comprehensive, there are still many minor subtleties you will discover over time.

# External References

— INTO SLAVE DIRECTORY
— CREATE 'TEMP' FILE
— 'SAVE AS' FROM SLAVE TO
                      TEM
— 'ERASE' MODEL SPACE' ALL'
— 'X REF' TO WORKING FIL
— INSERT 0,0
— SAVE AS 'TEMP' TO
— SLAVE FILE.

External References are vital to capitalizing on the power of AutoCAD. Those of you who've never investigated the XREF command, ask yourself the following questions:

- Have you ever wanted to temporarily reference another drawing from within your current drawing?
- Do you insert several detail drawings into one finished drawing?
- Do you create assemblies out of many different drawings?
- Are you constantly updating library symbols in different drawings?
- Do you find yourself inserting many drawings into one finished drawing only to end up with an incredibly large final drawing?
- Do you work in a workgroup situation that strives toward concurrent engineering?

If you answered yes to any of these questions, read on.

If you insert a wblock or block into your current drawing, you will get the entire block reference definition with it, even if you later delete the library symbol. Also, you'll be forced to purge your drawing to rid yourself of that extra garbage, even though you only wanted to use the drawing as a reference. External references to the rescue!

External references are exactly as their title indicates: externally referenced drawings. AutoCAD shoots a pointer out to the externally referenced drawing and brings the file into your current drawing. When you exit your drawing, AutoCAD releases the drawing, discarding all the excess baggage that goes along with the file. When you reenter your drawing, AutoCAD magically knows to go get the external reference again for your use. This process continues until you tell AutoCAD you are no longer interested in the externally referenced drawing. At that point, AutoCAD heartlessly casts it by the wayside.

To top that great feature, others are welcome to use the externally referenced drawing and make modifications to it. Each time AutoCAD goes out and gets the externally referenced drawing, you'll notice that all the new changes are incorporated within it.

The biggest and best benefit of using external references is that you can attach as many external references to your drawing as you want, without your base drawing getting any bigger!

You'll find the XREF command located under the Insert pulldown menu, along with its assorted options. If you'd like to follow along and try the various options, you'll need two drawings. One of the drawings we'll consider the base or current drawing, and the other drawing, we'll xref into the base drawing. The new XREF manager of Release 14 can be seen in Figure 1.

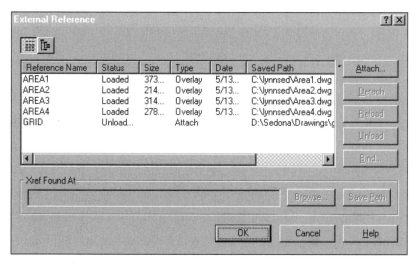

**Figure 1:** The External Reference Manager.

171

**Figure 2** The Attach Xref dialog box.

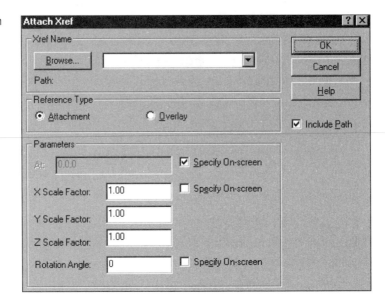

## Attaching an External Reference

The Attach option in the XREF command will send you to the Attach Xref dialog box as seen in Figure 2. It is used to form an official attachment of an external reference to a base drawing. This dialog will prompt you for the drawing you want to attach, as well as other parameters such as location. The options displayed are similar to to those found in the INSERT command (Scale factor, Rotation angle, and so on). You can key in the parameters, or specify them on-screen by checking the toggle button. You'll notice that the insertion point is relative to the origin of the xrefed drawing (unless a previous BASE point was selected). Select a drawing to attach to your base drawing, then select an insertion point, *x* and *y* scale factor, and rotation angle to complete the attachment. Hit OK to exit the dialog and you'll see your drawing appears in the XREF manager. When you exit the XREF manager, You'll see the referenced drawing within your base drawing.

Those of you in Release 12 will not get the nice file dialog box to help you select the name of the drawing you want to attach; you'll need to know the exact name to key in. You can also force a file dialog box by entering a tilde, ~, when prompted for the file name to attach.

So, what can you do with this externally referenced drawing? Treat it much like you would a block object. You can hatch it, snap to it, dimension it, use the inquiry commands on it, move it, and copy it. But you cannot modify or explode it. If you erase the xref, you'll also delete the object from your drawing but not the external reference definition. You must follow the proper procedure of DETACH to officially remove an xref from your drawing.

Let's take a look at your layers, or your block definitions. You'll notice that all of the layers from the externally referenced drawing kindly came along for the ride. The same is true for the block definitions and other named objects. Though you'll find the naming convention somewhat long for the externally referenced layers, you'll find them easy to distinguish from your existing layers. If we xrefed a drawing by the name of GEAR, you'd notice a group of layers similar to the following:

```
GEAR|CONST
GEAR|DETAILS
GEAR|DIM
```

If the drawing you xrefed had block definitions, the definitions will carry the same naming convention. If you go into the standard BLOCK command and list your blocks with the "?" option, you'll see something similar to the code shown in Listing 1.

---

**Listing 1.** Listing Blocks With "?"

```
Command: block
Block name (or ?): ?
Block(s) to list <*>:
Defined blocks.
   GEAR                        Xref: resolved
   GEAR|SPROCKET               Xdep: GEAR
User              External        Dependent        Unnamed
Blocks            References       Blocks           Blocks
0                 1               1                4
```

Dependent blocks are blocks that came along with the xref. You cannot use these dependent blocks unless you bind them to your drawing. (Note: Unnamed blocks are usually dimensions or hatch patterns. You may also notice that AutoCAD ignores block attributes in xrefs.)

You can control the visibility, color, and linetype of an xref's layer. But take note, by default, when you leave the base drawing, those values are reset to the original settings. This situation can be very frustrating if you go to great lengths to set up a particular layering scheme. Here is where the heroic visretain system variable comes to the rescue. When visretain is set to a value of 1 (which is, unfortunately, not the default), AutoCAD will remember all of your settings and store them for you. So, the next time you enter the base drawing, you'll see that the layers are exactly as you left them. Should you later decide to detach the external reference, however, all of these layers would vanish from your drawing. If you're on Release 14, you can find VISRETAIN in the details section of the Layer dialog box,

Save and exit your base drawing. Open the referenced drawing and make some obvious modifications. Exit the external reference drawing and reopen your base drawing. Are the modifications you just made reflected in your base drawing? You bet! External references can help ensure you're always viewing the most up-to-date information.

## Nesting External References (and Circular Xrefs)

Using xrefs to attach a drawing that contains its own xrefs is called "nesting external references." Technically, you can nest an xref if it contains a second xref that has a third xref that contains a fourth xref within a drawing. I'm sure you get the general idea. A problem does come into play, however, if you create a loop by xrefing into a drawing that already contains one or more of the nested xrefs. This situation is referred to as a circular external reference and will result in an warning message. It's difficult to explain, so let's look at a simplified example.

**1.** Drawing B has an xref attached to it called Drawing A.

**2.** You open Drawing A and use the XREF command to attach Drawing B.

This situation would create a circular xref along with a pleasant warning message.

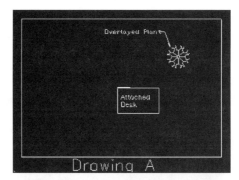

**Figure 3:** Drawing A, with one attached and one overlayed xref.

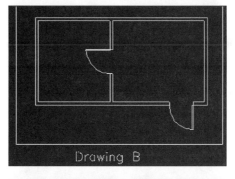

**Figure 4.** Drawing B (it has no xrefs).

## Overlaying External References (R13 and R14 only)

The inability to create circular external references has been a problem for the serious xref user. This issue prompted the creation of a new option called Overlay in the XREF command. The proper use of the Overlay option can eliminate the

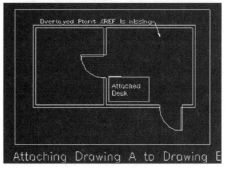

**Figure 5.** This figure shows the result of attached Drawing A and Drawing B.

circular reference problem altogether. Follow this simple scenario:

**1.** Drawing B has an xref attached to it called Drawing A.

**2.** You decide to attach Drawing B to Drawing C. Will you be able to see the xref Drawing A? Definitely.

**3.** Attach Drawing C to Drawing D. While you're in Drawing D, you'll be able to see Drawing A, B, and C. All of the xrefs follow the base drawing wherever it might go. They are inseparable unless they are officially detached.

175

However, an overlayed xref doesn't follow the Base drawing wherever it goes. It resides in the base drawing only. If the base drawing is attached to another drawing, you won't see the overlayed xref in the final drawing. Let's try another example to illustrate this point:

**1.** Drawing B has an overlayed xref called Drawing A.

**2.** You decide to attach Drawing B to Drawing C. Will you be able to see Drawing A? No, you won't. Drawing A stayed behind.

Reflecting back on our example of a circular xref, if you changed the original attachment to an overlay, AutoCAD won't return an error message.

Other than this operation, an overlayed xref has the same properties and functionality as an attached xref. You're not missing out on anything by using the Overlay option versus the Attach option. To overlay an XREF, you'd select the Overlay option in the Attach Xref dialog box.

## Detaching or Binding an External Reference

When you're finished using the external reference, you can detach it from your base drawing (never erase!), which will remove all of its layer and block references as well.

Should you decide to keep an xref for good (perhaps for editing purposes), you can use the Bind option in the XREF command. The Bind option requires that you key in the name of the xref that you want to bind (don't bother picking from the screen, it will ignore you). After binding an external reference, you'll find it takes on the properties of a wblock. You can now explode and modify the external reference objects. Once you bind an xref, you will no longer see any modifications made in the original xrefed drawing. The link has been broken.

The layer and block names are somewhat different as well. Let's take a look at the new layering name convention:

```
GEAR$0$CONST
GEAR$0$DETAILS
GEAR$0$DIM
```

You'll want to change the name of these layers pronto; they're too long and scary looking! If you are going to give drawings that contain external references to clients, be sure to Bind the xrefs before handing it over. Otherwise, your clients will be frustrated when they open your drawings to find all of the xrefs missing. They're living happily at home on your computer.

Release 14 added an additional option that may be preferred over Binding an XREF. The new Insert option allows you to simply change the XREF to a block definition, thus eliminating the lengthy layer names. This new option is found in the XREF manager.

## Changing the Path and Reloading your External References

When you attach or overlay an external reference, AutoCAD remembers the path and the directory where it was stored. AutoCAD always looks in this directory first, when searching for the xref to load. Should you move the xrefed drawing to another directory, you really should let AutoCAD know! This step is extremely crucial when you're working in a network environment where individuals may be mapped to different drives. If AutoCAD cannot find the xref drawing in its original directory, it will also search the AutoCAD support path set up using the acad environment variable. If you've set up a Project in the Preferences dialog box, AutoCAD will search your project directories as well.

Let's say you're working in an environment where concurrent engineering is prevalent. You could be working on a floor plan at the same time the electrical engineer is working on the electrical system of the building. You've already xrefed the electrical drawing into the floor plan when they tell you that some changes have been made. The Reload option will go back and get the drawing again, reloading it with the most recent modifications. It definitely beats exiting and reloading the drawing.

This explanation is a fairly high-level one of the world of external references. If you want to investigate further, look into clipping external references using the new XCLIP command or xbinding any of the named objects that belong to your external reference. For example, the xref you brought into your base object has a great chair you'd like to have access to in your base drawing. You might even want to be able to modify it. The XBIND command can be used for this very purpose. XCLIP allows you to clip away portions of your external reference you don't wish to display.

I remember doing some work with the city of Glendale, CA, a few years ago. They had one monster drawing of the city that was so huge that it took about 15 minutes just to regenerate and display on the screen. This enormous map was actually a combination of about 30 different drawings inserted into one final drawing, resulting in the enormous file size. Not only was it a behemoth, but each time they made a modification to one of the individual drawings, they also had to remember to update the map of the entire city.

Switching so that they could use external references made their lives dramatically easier. Their drawing was no longer out of control and, as they updated the individual xrefed drawings, those changes were automatically made in the final combination map of the city.

External references are used extensively by AutoCAD power users. So, find out why they are vital to so many industry professionals. Give them a try!

# Calculating Geometries

Precision is important to an AutoCAD operator, and AutoCAD provides many methods to insure your drawings are geometrically and mathematically accurate. The underused and somewhat complex Geometric Calculator is one of the powerful tools AutoCAD has to define specific points and values in your drawing. We'll digest the online Geometric Calculator capabilities in small, simple doses, and you'll wonder how you ever used AutoCAD without it!

Available since Release 11, the CAL command actually came to us as an AutoLISP routine. The CAL command can be used to solve mathematical problems or locate specific points in a drawing. The code the CAL command uses is somewhat cryptic and tends to send the casual user running for cover. Power AutoCAD users know only too well how powerful the CAL command is.

The CAL command evaluates expressions. You can use the Geometric Calculator in much the same way as you use a hand-held calculator (though I wouldn't want to balance my check book with it!). CAL is available transparently (from within another command) by preceding the command with an apostrophe. We'll start with some simple mathematical expressions.

## Mathematical Expressions

CAL uses the standard mathematical rules of precedence. Do you remember the phrase "Please Excuse My Dear Aunt Sally"? No doubt one of your math teachers taught you this phrase to illustrate the abbreviation of Parentheses, Exponents, Multiplication, Division, Addition, and Subtraction. The CAL command solves expressions using this order of precedence. The following mathematical symbols are used and understood by the Geometric Calculator:

( ) Parenthesis are used to group expressions (**P**lease).

^  This symbol indicates an exponent, for example: 5^3 is the same as 5 to the 3rd power or 5 cubed (125) (**E**xcuse).

\*  An asterisk indicates multiplication, for example: 5\*3 is the same as 5 times 3 or 15 (**M**y).

/  A forward slash indicates division, for example: 9/3 is the same as 9 divided by 3 or 3 (**D**ear).

+  A plus sign indicates addition (**A**unt).

-  A minus sign indicates subtraction (**S**ally).

Here's how it works using the Calculator:

```
Command: CAL
Initializing...>> Expression: 5*3
15
Command: CAL >> Expression: 8*(4/2)
16.0
Command: CAL >> Expression: 5^3
125.0
```

Now, there's no need to find your calculator when you need to perform a mathematical function on the fly. (By the way, the Geometric Calculator accepts *pi* as the constant value 3.14159.) Let's take a look at some of the more sophisticated numeric functions (those of you who are allergic to math can skip to the next section!):

• **sin (angle)** returns the sine of the indicated angle, for example: **sin(90)** returns the value 1.

- **cos (angle)** returns the cosine of the indicated angle.
- **tang (angle)** returns the tangent of the angle.
- **asin (angle)** returns the arcsine of the indicated number. The indicated number must be between -1 and 1 (Can you remember those evil sine waves from high school?). For example, asin (1) returns 90 degrees; arcsine means the angle who's sine is 1.
- **acos(angle)** returns the arccosine of the number (same restrictions as asin).
- **atan(angle)** returns the arctangent of the number.
- **ln(real)** returns the natural log of a number (to the base e).
- **log(real)** returns the log (to the base 10) of the number that is indicated.
- **sqr (real)** returns the square of a number. For example: **sqr(5)** returns 25.
- **sqrt(real)** returns the square root of a number. For example: **sqrt(100)** returns 10.
- **r2d(angle)** (Radians to Degrees) returns the indicated angle (in radians ) in degrees.
- **d2r(angle)** (Degrees to Radians) returns the indicated angle to radians.

## Units and Angles Format

If you want to use feet and inches with the calculator, you'll need to use the proper syntax. The two acceptable formats are: feet'-inches" or feet'inches", or 2'-6" or 2'6".

The calculator will convert these values to real numbers (based on inches). For example: 2'6" will convert to 30 and 8" will convert to 8.

CAL also assumes you'll be using degrees for input. You can, however, specify radians with an **r** and grads with a **g**. You can also specify minutes and seconds (but you'll have to use a delimiter of **d**). For example: 130.2r is equal to 130.2 radians, 15d10'25" is equal to 15 degrees, 10 minutes and 25 seconds, and 16g is equal to 16 grads. Regardless of your input, the calculator converts the value to degrees.

## Points

The Geometric Calculator can also handle points. Points, locations in space, are defined via an $x,y,z$ value—just as they are in AutoCAD. The Geometric Calculator expects points to be enclosed within brackets [ ]:

```
Command: LINE From point: 'cal
>> Expression: [2,2]
to point: 'cal
>> Expression: [6,0]
```

AutoCAD assumes a value of 0 if it's not included, for example: [1,,3] is the same as (1,0,3); [,,2] is evaluated to (0,0,2). Wouldn't it be nice if AutoCAD accepted coordinate input the same way?

Polar, cylindrical, spherical, and relative coordinates are also accepted using the standard AutoCAD syntax. For example:

```
>> Expression: [@2<45<30] (relative-spherical)
```

So why go to all this trouble? Stay tuned, we'll put this all together and you'll begin to see the true benefits.

## Vectors

By definition, any two points define a vector. After defining a vector, you can find out the direction and length of that vector. See the following code as an example:

```
>>Expression: vec ([1,2],[3,4])
(2.0 2.0 0.0)
```

The value returned is the distance traveled in the $x$ from the first point followed by the distance in the $y$ and $z$. To calculate the distance between the two points:

```
>>Expression: dist ([1,2],[3,4])
```

## Finding the Radius of an Arc or Circle

Perhaps you'd like to draw a circle that's one-third the size of
an existing circle. Using the calculator, you can find the radius
of an existing circle, then divide the result by three (or multiply
by one-third). For example:

```
Command: CIRCLE
3P/2P/TTR/<Center point>: cen
of Diameter/<Radius> <0.7910>: 'cal
>> Expression: rad/3
>> Select circle, arc or polyline segment for RAD
   function:
```

It will automatically draw another circle at the indicated
point that's one-third the size of the original.

## Object Snaps

The calculator can prompt for a particular object snap within an
expression as well. Here's a list of the proper syntax for calling
an object snap:

- **END**      Endpoint
- **INS**      Insertion point
- **INT**      Intersection
- **MID**      Midpoint
- **CEN**      Center
- **NEA**      Nearest
- **NOD**      Node (point)
- **QUA**      Quadrant
- **PER**      Perpendicular
- **TAN**      Tangent

(Note that the new **from** and **apparent** intersection object
snaps are not accepted by the calculator.) These object snaps
always return a point value (*x,y,z*). The result is saved under the
AutoCAD system variable **lastpoint**. Also, use the @ to reference the result in the next drawing or editing command. To
pick a point on the screen without using object snaps while in

183

the Calculator command, use the **cur** function. It prompts you for a point.

Here is where the calculator becomes very powerful. Let's say I wanted to find the midpoint between the center of a circle and the endpoint of a line:

```
(cen+end)/2
```

You will be prompted to select an arc or circle first (it will record the coordinates for the center point). As shown in Figure 1. Then, it will prompt you to select an object with an endpoint (it will record the coordinates for the endpoint). It takes those two coordinates and divides them by two to find the midpoint. Without the calculator, you'd probably create construction lines to find this value.

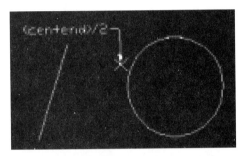

**Figure 1:** Using the calculator to find the midpoint between the center of a circle and the endpoint of a line.

How about the center (centroid) of a triangle? Construct a triangle and try this great equation:

```
(end+end+end)/3
```

The Geometric Calculator will prompt for the three corners of the triangle, divide those values by three, and find the center for you. As shown in Figure 2.

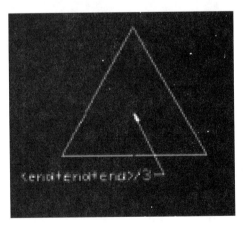

**Figure 2:** Using the calculator to find the centroid of a triangle.

## Using Variables

The Geometric Calculator can also set and read variables, allowing us to temporarily store specific points, numeric values, or vectors for use later on in the drawing session. Let's set some simple variables:

```
Command:
CAL >> Expression: x=1
1 (AutoCAD returns the value)
Command:
CAL >> Expression: y=2
2
Command:
CAL >> Expression: x+y
3
```

You can also assign points and vectors to variables:

```
Command: CAL
>> Expression: pt1=[2,3]
(2.0 3.0 0.0)
```

These expressions set **pt1** to the value (2,3).

Let's make it more difficult. My goal is to create a tooling hole one unit over and up from the center of an existing circle. First, I'll use the calculator to set a variable of a point one unit up and one unit over from the center of my circle.

```
Command: cal
>> Expression: pt2=cen+[1,1]
>> Select entity for CEN snap:
(13.7172 7.19474 0.0)
```

Now, I'll use **pt2** as the center of my new tooling hole:

```
Command: CIRCLE
3P/2P/TTR/<Center point>: 'cal
>> Expression: pt2
Diameter/<Radius> <3.6048>:
```

Incidentally, I could have performed this entire operation at once by accessing CAL twice from within the CIRCLE command.

## Shortcut Functions

The Geometric Calculator has included shortcut functions for some commonly used expressions. These functions provide information quickly and easily. I've included the ones I feel are the most valuable in everyday drafting:

- **DEE** is a shortcut for Distance, End, End. It returns the distance between two endpoints on one or two objects.
- **ILLE** is a shortcut for Intersection, Line, Line, Endpoint. It's used to find the intersection point between two lines. You will be prompted for all four endpoints of the two lines.
- **MEE** is a shortcut for Midpoint, End, End. It finds the midpoint between any two endpoints, as shown in Figure 3.

**Figure 3:** MEE—
Midpoint, End, End.

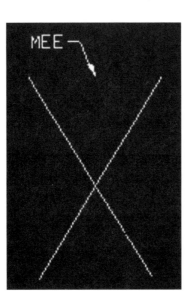

We've covered about half of the capabilities of the CAL command. It takes practice and clever thinking to increase productivity using it.

# AutoCAD Filters

By definition, a filter is similar to a sieve, in that it is used to sift or sort things. AutoCAD has several different types of filters to help you sort through objects, coordinates, and layers (just to name a few).

Have you ever worked on a drawing created by a coworker with bad CAD habits, only to find that little or no layering standards were used? Perhaps you were working on a Rush and neglected to place the text on the TEXT layer or dimensions on the DIM layer? Have you ever wanted to quickly erase all your construction points and lines? Using the many object-selection methods in AutoCAD, you can usually grab the desired objects quickly and easily—if they conveniently lie in close proximity of each other and no other objects are in the way. Wouldn't you like to be able to sort objects by name, layer, color, and so forth rather than by visually selecting them on the screen? The FILTER command in AutoCAD is an incredibly powerful tool that can help you in all of these scenarios. AutoLISPers know all too well the power of filtering. Knowing nothing about AutoLISP, however, we can still use the FILTER command to harness this power ourselves.

The FILTER command (which happens to be transparent) sends you to a dialog box, shown in Figure 1, which contains a plethora of options.

The object behind the FILTER command is to create a set of criteria to be used to create a selection set. Perhaps you'd like

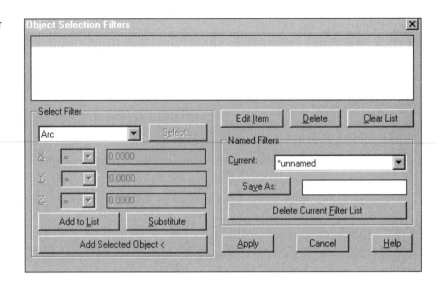

**Figure 1:** The Filter Dialog Box.

AutoCAD to search for all the circles in your drawing, or all the blue circles, or all the blue circles with a radius of 1. You can create any set of rules you'd like AutoCAD to follow when it goes on its search. Let's start by taking a look at the various possible filters you can select. In the Filter dialog box, select the word "Arc" underneath the words "Select Filter."

## Object Type

You can choose to filter by object type. You'll see the name of all the different types of objects in AutoCAD, such as Arc, Circle, Dimension, and Point.

## Properties

Along with object type, we have the obvious need for Property filters. Properties, such as Color, Layer, and Linetype, are useful ways of filtering out specific objects. Selecting a property requires more definition than the object type. If you select Layer, you need to define which layer; if you select Color, you'll need to define which color; and so on. After selecting a property, you'll notice that the "Select..." button is enabled. Use this button to select the actual property you want to filter. Properties available include Color, Elevation, Layer, Linetype, and Thickness (extrusion).

## Individual Object Characteristics

Rather than defining a broad category, such as object type, you might choose to narrow down the physical characteristics about a particular type of object. Rather than merely filtering with the definition of Circle, you can select all the Circles with a Radius of 3. You'll notice that many of the object types contain even more differentiating categories. For example, let's look at TEXT. You could filter text by position (the coordinates of the location of specific text), value (actual characters), style name, height, or rotation. That's quite a few filters for one object type. Some objects have many filters; some only have one.

I've outlined them as listed in the dialog box. It's interesting to note that they are not necessarily alphabetized.

Objects listed with no further filters include body, leader, polyline, ray, region, solid, solid body, spline, trace (do any of you still use this command?), 3dface, tolerance, and xline. I find it surprising that there aren't any additional Polyline filters (such as, width). There's even a Filter for Xdata ID. The miscellaneous filter of Normal Vector references the normal to the UCS in which the object was drawn (incredibly important for the mechanical world).

Some of the object-type filters require more information. For example, Arc Radius. Below the listbox are three text boxes labeled X, Y, and Z. Should you be prompted for a real number, such as Radius, you'll include that input in the X region. Y and Z will be grayed out leaving the X box enabled. If you're filtering a value, such as a coordinate position, you can place a value in all three boxes. Even if you need to specify a filter, such as text value or dimension style, you'll put the name in the X box. (Is it just me or have you all noticed that the Y box looks off center?)

**Figure 2**

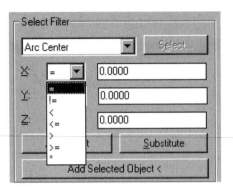

You could also choose to be even more creative with your filter. Perhaps you'd like to filter out all the circles with a radius larger than three. Notice the = pull-down list that is positioned right next to the coordinate (see Figure 2).

You'll recognize the obvious less-than (<), greater-than (>), less-than or equal to (<=), and greater-than or equal to (>=) symbols. What about != and *? The != is used to signify "NOT equal to" and the asterisk is used as a standard wildcard for all possibilities. If you want to *really* test someone's knowledge of the intricacies of AutoCAD, ask them if they know what the != signifies in the FILTER command. If they get it right, they're truly a certifiable AutoCAD Wizard. Let's look at a few examples. If you'd like to select all the circles with a radius equal to or larger than 3.5, you'd use X >= 3.5. For all of the circles that do not have a radius of 7.6 use X != 7.6. To find all of the circles with any radius use X *.

The asterisk doesn't make much sense to me because I normally select an object type of Circle and not Circle Radius to select all circles. I also noticed that if you selected Arc Radius and used the wildcard * to indicate all possibilities that Auto-CAD found all the Arcs and all the Circles in the drawing. The Radius filter just wandered through and found all objects with a radius, regardless of object type.

As you select your filters, be sure to include them in the Filter list by picking the button that says "Add to list." A common mistake is to go straight to Apply without saving the filter to a list. Each time you select "Add to list," you'll see the new filter appear in the box below the title "Object Selection Filters."

Your filter selection set can become quite complex with the additional filter options available at the end of the filter list. If you've done any programming, the And, Or, and Not options will make complete sense. For those of you who've preferred to stay as far from programming as possible (wise choice), I'll run through these valuable, and really quite simple, options.

The first rule is to balance the options. If you have a Begin And, you must also have an End And. If you have a Begin Not, you must also have an End Not, and so forth.

Let's say you wanted to select the Ellipses that were the Color Blue or on Layer "Construct." Select the Object type of Ellipse, follow this with a **Begin Or, select the filter of Color Blue followed by the other Filter of Layer Construct, and complete it with the **End Or. It should look similar to the following code:

```
Object =Ellipse
**Begin OR
Color  =5-Blue
Layer  =CONSTRUCT
**End OR
```

If you wanted all the Text that did not have a height of 1.5:

```
Object =Text
**Begin NOT
Text Height   =1.5000
**End NOT
```

I haven't found much use for And because, by default, the Filter dialog box assumes the selection set must satisfy all the filters (equivalent to And). And XOr appears to do the same thing as Or (help me out if you've been able to find a good use of XOr over Or!).

Let's review the remaining buttons in the dialog box. Edit Item is used to make changes to an item you've already placed in the List box. After making the necessary changes, select the Substitute button to make the replacement. If you select Add to List after editing the item, you'll add an additional filter to the filter list; Delete will remove the highlighted item from the Filter List; and Clear List returns you to a clean slate because it removes all of the entries in the filter list.

191

If you regularly use a complicated filter list, why not save it to a file. AutoCAD creates a filter-list file called *filter.nfl* (named filter list). You can save and retrieve filter selections by name to or from this file (up to 18 characters). The Delete Filter List button is used to delete a filter list from the *filter.nfl* file.

The coolest button in the dialog box is Add Selected Object. This button is a quick-and-dirty way to create a complete filter list. Select an object that contains most of the qualities you're looking for in your selection set. AutoCAD will fill the Filter List section with all the data about that object. Then it's up to you to delete out the filters you don't want included. The deletion process is a little tedious because the dialog box doesn't recognize the <Shift> key as a viable means to select many entries at once. Regardless, this option can prove to be a very efficient means to an end.

So, you've created your filter list, now what do you do? Select the Apply button and put a window around all the objects you want your criteria to be used on. AutoCAD will return the number of objects it considered, and the number it filtered out after applying the filter. The difference between the two values is the actual number of objects it selected. The objects that successfully pass the test will be put into the current selection set. You can also use the object selection option of "All" to put all the objects in your drawing (except those on a Frozen layer) to the test.

How do you use these objects? Enter the editing command of your choice and use **P** for Previous to recall the selection set found in the FILTER command. Only the objects that pass your filtering criteria should highlight.

Because the FILTER command is transparent, you should feel free to use it during an editing command. When prompted to select objects, enter the FILTER command, set up your filters, and hit Apply. If you are manually keying the FILTER command, don't forget the apostrophe.

The FILTER command is an extremely underused yet valuable tool. Be creative and expand your horizons—the FILTER command can really help you save time!

# Positive Attributes

Library symbols (blocks), in and of themselves, are not very intelligent. They have so much potential if defined properly, but we tend to produce the same old witless blocks day after day. We'll strive to raise the IQ of our library symbols by assigning a variety of attributes to them.

Are you still inserting empty title blocks only to fill them out later with ordinary text? Do you find yourself prone to independently align and size each text string? I've even seen the opposite extreme of inserting a dummy title block prefilled with text and later exploding it to replace the existing text with the proper drawing information. You're working entirely too hard.

If you have ever found yourself in a situation where you have a library symbol with text that varies from insertion to insertion, you should seriously take a look at using Attributes. Title blocks, balloons, and standard symbols also come to mind. Attributes can also be used in a more advanced manner by extracting the data from the drawing. You could, in effect, create a bill of materials using the information you've attached to your blocks. Attributes can definitely save you time and energy in the long run—but there's a catch. Attributes require planning up front, before you create your library symbols.

We'll work with an incredibly simple title block that will contain four attributes. Our finished title block, including information, will look like Figure 1.

193

**Figure 1:** Title block with attributes.

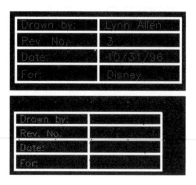

**Figure 2:** Title block template.

Begin by creating a template of a title block. Create the simple grid of lines shown along with some simple text, as shown in Figure 2. The attributes we define will be placed in the right half of the title block. The four definitions we'll create are called:

- NAME: The name of the person who created the drawing.
- REVNO: The revision number of the drawing.
- DATE: The date of this revision.
- CLIENT: The customer the drawing was created for.

To assign an attribute definition, we'll use the DDATTDEF command. The age-old command-prompt-driven ATTDEF command is too archaic for my liking, but you're welcome to explore it. In AutoCAD Release 14, the dialog box for creating attribute definitions is located in the Draw =>Block pull-down menu under Define Attribute. . ., as shown in Figure 3.

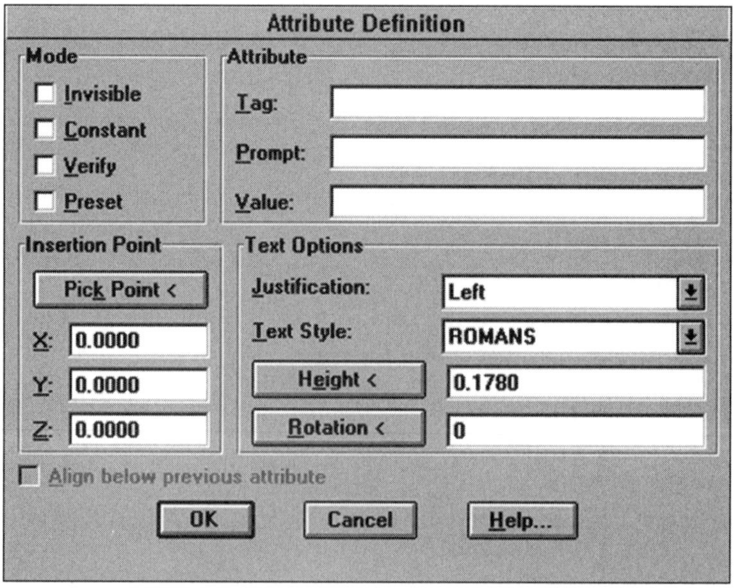

**Figure 3:** Attribute Definition dialog box (DDATTDEF).

194

As we create our first attribute definition, we'll dissect this dialog box section by section.

## Attribute Modes

There are four different attribute modes that can be assigned to an attribute. These modes are completely optional. Depending on the type of attribute you're creating, you may choose to toggle on one or more of these modes.

**Invisible:** Fairly self-explanatory, the Invisible mode controls whether or not the attribute value is displayed or not. For example, if we were to toggle this mode ON for the NAME attribute, the name of the person who created the drawing would never display in our title block. This mode is useful in situations where we want to record some information with one of our library symbols but don't want to display it for the world to see. A cost attribute of a part, a salary of an employee, and so on are good examples of potential invisible attributes. In facilities management, imagine a block of a computer that has invisible attributes of an asset tag number, make, model, and configuration. We don't really have attributes in our title block that need to be invisible, but we'll set the REVNO attribute to invisible just for experimentation purposes.

**Constant:** Should you choose to assign a value that never changes, you can do so with Constant. It is primarily used by those who extract the attribute information from their drawings. A constant attribute might be the name of a vendor you always use for a particular part or the fixed name of a part. A Constant attribute can never be modified. Because we have no intention of extracting the data from our title block, we'll leave this toggled OFF.

**Verify:** Verify is useful if you're inputting complicated numeric values that are easily mistyped. These values might be parts numbers or social security numbers. Verify will reprompt you for the attribute value, displaying the value you've already keyed in. Just for practice, we'll toggle Verify ON for our date attribute.

195

**Preset:** This mode is one of the newer additions to the ATTDEF command. Preset has the look and feel of the Constant mode but with the additional capability of being able to modify the attribute at some later date. Preset uses the value assigned to it as the default. We'll toggle Preset ON for our Client attribute.

## The Attribute Section

This section contains the meat of the dialog. Here, we will assign the name of the attribute tag, which is the prompt we give to the user and the default value.

**Tag:** The attribute tag is the official name of the attribute. This value is critical for attribute extraction, as it would be the value we would call to. If you explode a block with attributes assigned to it, the tag will display instead of the value. We will assign "Name" as the attribute tag. Though it isn't case sensitive, AutoCAD will convert the tag to uppercase. The tag can contain any characters except for spaces.

**Prompt:** You get to play the role of programmer and decide what you'd like the prompt to be for your attribute. This part is often hard to grasp. When you insert your title block, AutoCAD will prompt the user for information. A good prompt for Name might be "Drawing by" or "Enter the person's name who created this drawing." You get the opportunity to make your CAD program as friendly or abusive as you'd like! Obviously, spaces are permissible.

**Value:** This is the default attribute value. Just as AutoCAD is laced with defaults, you get the responsibility of deciding your own default attribute value. If I were the primary user of this title block, I'd probably use my name as the default. If I were creating a custom title block for another user, I'd probably put that user's name in as the default. See Figure 4 for an example of values you can choose to put in the attribute section.

At this point, all that's left is to decide where you want the attribute to be placed within your title block and the properties of the text (height, style, rotation angle, and so forth).

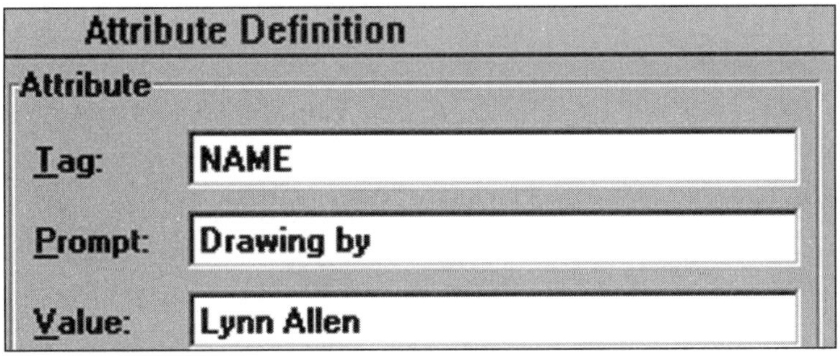

**Figure 4:** "Name" attribute definition.

## Insertion Point

On the lower left corner of the dialog box, you'll see an option for an insertion point. Unless you know the exact coordinates of where you'd like the attribute to go, you'll need to select the Pick point option to manually show where to place the attribute. If, by some remote chance, you do know the coordinates, you can key them into the appropriate x, y, and z boxes. Use the Pick Point option to select a point in the upper-right box of your title block.

## Text Options

The Text Options section of the ATTDEF dialog box controls the rotation angle, text style, text height, and justification. Pulling this section out of the ATTDEF dialog box would make a great DTEXT dialog. These options are fairly self-explanatory, so I won't dwell on them; they follow basic text rules. There's a small, yet significant, option in the lower-left-hand corner of the dialog box that reads "Align below previous attribute." If you're lining up several attributes, one beneath the other, this option places them neatly using standard text spacing.

After picking OK to exit the dialog box, the attribute tag will display in the title box. Create the remaining attributes using the values indicated in Figures 5 through 7. Toggle ON the Invisible mode. Toggle Verify ON for the DATE attribute (don't forget to toggle OFF the Invisible mode). Toggle Preset ON for the CLIENT attribute (and OFF the Verify mode). When you're finished assigning your attributes, your display should look like Figure 8.

Now, we'll use the BLOCK command to save our hard work. Of course, if you planned on creating a library symbol you plan on keeping, you'd use the WBLOCK command. Enter the BLOCK command and follow along:

```
Command: BLOCK
Block name (or ?): TITLE
```

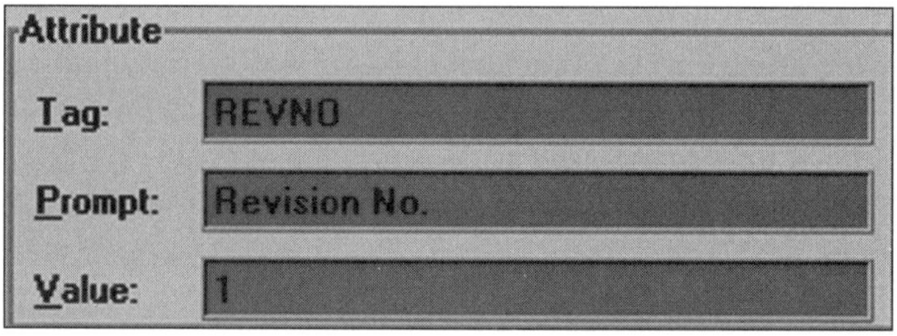

**Figure 5:** "Revision No." attribute definition.

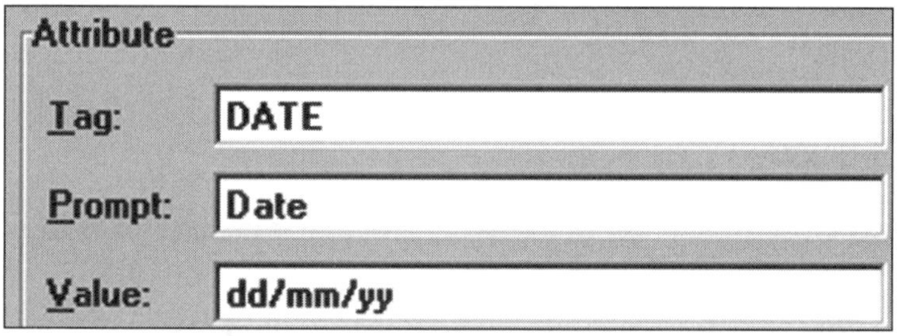

**Figure 6:** "Date" attribute definition.

**Figure 7:** "Client" attribute definition box.

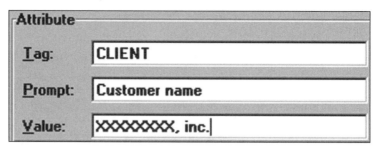

**Figure 8:** Title block with attribute values (before saving).

```
Insertion base point: int (pick the corner you'd like to
   use as your insertion point)
of
Select objects: STOP!
```

The order in which you select the objects saved in your block will determine the order the INSERT command prompts for your attribute values. If you window all of your objects, the chances are the attributes will display in reverse order. In other words, AutoCAD will ask you for Customer name, followed by the Date, Revision Number, and lastly, Name. I'm sure we'd prefer our attributes to prompt in the order they're listed in our title block. So here's the magical tip of the day: Manually select the attributes in the order you want them to display. Using Windows to select attribute values leaves the order up to the discretion of the computer! We will window all of the objects except for the attributes, then select them individually from the top to the bottom.

Now, you're ready to insert your title block. Notice as you insert the block, that our DATE attribute reprompts us to ensure that we keyed in the proper date. The CLIENT attribute didn't prompt us at all, but assumed the default, and the REVNO value is invisible.

## Displaying Your Attributes in a Dialog Box

By default, AutoCAD displays attributes using the Command: prompt interface, which is just not very friendly. The powerful system variable **attdia** will make inserting our attributes much easier. When **attdia** is set to 1, our attributes will display in a dialog box making them easier to set and modify, as shown in Figure 9. I think you'll agree that this method is much more user friendly.

To display all of the attributes regardless of their visibility settings, we use the ATTDISP command. There are three options in this command: Normal, ON, and OFF. Normal uses the visibility settings stored with the block, ON displays all of the attributes,

199

and OFF turns them all off. Turn ATTDISP to ON to display the REVNO attribute in your title block.

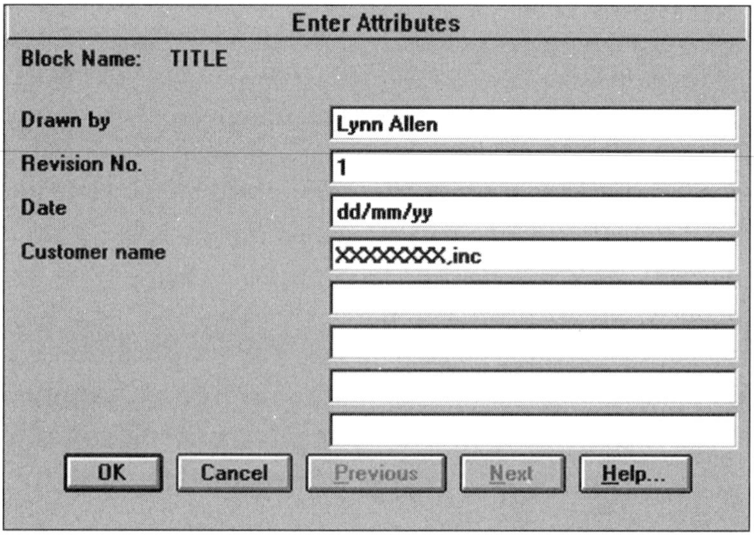

**Figure 9:** Enter Attributes dialog box.

## Enter Attributes

**Block Name:** TITLE

| | |
|---|---|
| Drawn by | Lynn Allen |
| Revision No. | 1 |
| Date | dd/mm/yy |
| Customer name | XXXXXXXX,inc |

OK    Cancel    Previous    Next    Help...

After inserting blocks with attributes, you may need to edit the attribute values. There are two commands that are used to edit attributes: DDATTE and ATTEDIT.

• DDATTE. The simplest method of editing attribute values is to use the DDATTE command. This command places a dialog box on the screen displaying all of the attribute values. Simply make modifications to any of the displayed attributes. DDATTE is located in the Modify pull-down menu of R14 under Object=>Attribute=>Single. R12 users will spend a little extra time finding it in the Draw pull-down menu under Text, Attributes, Edit. (Remember, you can't edit the value of constant attributes.)

DDATTE only permits editing the attribute values. If you choose to edit other characteristics, such as height, position, or rotation angle, use the ATTEDIT command. If you need to make a global modification to many attributes, ATTEDIT will also come into play.

- ATTEDIT. Located under the Modify pull-down menu under Object=>Attribute=>Global, the ATTEDIT command has many more options and capabilities. R12 users will need to key in this command since it's not located within the pull-down menus. Because ATTEDIT is strictly a command-line interface command, it's typically used only when DDATTE doesn't do the trick. You'll also notice that some archaic structure still exists within this command. Let's look at ATTEDIT:

```
Command: ATTEDIT
Edit attributes one at a time? <Y>
```

There are two paths you can follow in the ATTEDIT command: editing your attributes globally (affecting multiple attributes) or one at a time. We'll follow the default path of one at a time for starters.

- Block name specification <*>: If you are only interested in making changes to one type of block, key in the block name here. This setup will limit your selection set to only those attributes that pertain to the designated block. For example, say you want to change the attribute text height on a few of your doors. Specifying that you're interested only in the block name of Door would eliminate accidentally getting windows or miscellaneous furniture within your selection set. If you press [Enter] to accept the default of *, all blocks will be taken into consideration when you physically select the attributes to be edited.
- Attribute tag specification <*>: You can choose to further narrow your selection set of attributes by specifying a particular attribute tag. For example, your Door block has four attributes in it. Let's say you're only interested in changing the text height on one of those attribute tags, namely type. If you specify that you are only interested in the type attribute, you could avoid also including the other three attributes within your selection set. Essentially, this could save you time later on in the ATTEDIT command. Users who have drawings filled with blocks and attributes find these specifications quite

201

useful. If you accept the default of *, all attribute tags will be taken into consideration when you select the attributes to be edited.

- Attribute value specification <*>: If you really want to narrow down your choices within a selection set, indicate a specific attribute value—for example, say you only want to make modifications to the text height of any attribute values that say "Firedoor." That's pretty specific! Once again, if you accept the default of *, all attribute values will be taken into consideration when you select the attributes to be edited. Now, we're ready to physically select our attributes. (Note: Any of these answers will accept wildcard combinations. For example, B* would select all of the values that begin with the letter B.)

- Select Attributes: I must admit, ATTEDIT took a minor step backwards with R13. It only granted us one chance to select the attributes we want to edit. Previous releases would let us pick and pick and pick, until we indicated we were finished by hitting that final [Enter]. R13 apparently has more faith in our proper selection capabilities (though perhaps that faith is misplaced). Release 14 gives us back that second chance so many of us need.

After selecting your attributes, AutoCAD will indicate the number of attributes you selected. One of the attributes will be highlighted and an X will appear at the insertion point of that attribute. This indicates the attribute you're currently editing. Let's review the available options:

**Value/Position/Height/Angle/Style/Layer/Color/Next <N>:**

- **Value:** Long before there were dialog boxes and DDATTE, this option was the only means of changing an attribute value. Now, it's much easier to use the Attribute Edit dialog box (DDATTE) for changing a value:

```
Change or Replace? <R>:
New attribute value:
```

Should you choose Replace, you'll be prompted for a new string to replace the entire value. The other option, Change, is somewhat more involved and works much like the standard Search and Replace:

```
String to change: a
New string: e
```

This would replace every a in the attribute value with an e. It is also case sensitive.

- **Position:** This option permits moving the attribute value to a new location.
- **Height:** This option is used to modify the existing text height of the attribute value.
- **Angle:** This option is used to modify the text rotation angle.
- **Style:** You can use this option to change the text style of the attribute value. You must select an existing text style.
- **Layer:** If you'd like to change the layer that the attribute value is placed on, key in the name of the new layer.
- **Color:** This option is used to change the color of the attribute value.
- **Next (default):** When it is finished modifying the current attribute value, Next will bring you to the next selected attribute. This attribute will be highlighted with an X to ensure you're aware of the attribute you're changing.

Remember, you're only changing the various properties of one attribute value in one block. These changes don't affect any other attributes.

Let's re-enter the ATTEDIT command and take the Global route:

```
Command: ATTEDIT
Edit attributes one at a time? <Y> n
Global edit of attribute values.
Edit only attributes visible on screen? <Y>
```

You would enter "No" if you wanted AutoCAD to consider editing invisible attributes as well.

```
Block name specification <*>:
Attribute tag specification <*>:
Attribute value specification <*>:
Select Attributes:
6 attributes selected.
String to change:
New string:
```

Notice a key difference from editing attributes one at a time. You are able to modify only the attribute value using this method. Any modification you enter under New String will affect all of the selected attributes. This method is the fastest making an attribute value change to many attributes. For example, you input a part number of C3406 for 20 blocks. That part number is discontinued and replaced with an updated part with a number of D3406. Global editing could quickly replace all of the Cs to Ds.

## Redefining Blocks with Attributes

So, what do you do when you need to change the position of all of your type attributes in your Door block, including those you want to insert in the future? What if you need to add another attribute to a library symbol after you've already inserted several in your current drawing?

Should you realize that you actually need to modify the original block containing attributes, you'll need to take yet a different approach. Making attribute modifications to a block you haven't inserted yet, however, is pretty simple. Here's the step-by-step approach:

1. Insert the block.
2. Explode the block.
3. Modify or add to the attributes accordingly (DDMODIFY comes in handy here).
4. Reblock the part.

These four steps will update the block definition, and the changes will be made. If you need to make attribute modifications to a block you've already inserted, the procedure is somewhat more complicated. If you use the preceding method to

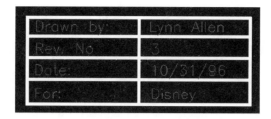

**Figure 10:** Inserted title block with attribute values.

modify the block, you'll find that none of the previously inserted attributes will update. If you add new attributes to the block, they won't show on the existing blocks either, which makes the command ATTREDEF necessary for redefining attributes.

## ATTREDEF

ATTREDEF initially existed as a LISP routine. If you have R12 or a previous release, load the routine first. It can be done by using the APPLOAD dialog box under the File pull-down menu, Applications. ATTREDEF is located in the Sample directory. R13 users will find it under the Modify pull-down menu under Attribute, Redefine. R14 users will need to key in the command (it's been removed from the pull-down menus).

ATTREDEF is used in place of the BLOCK command to redefine your block with attributes. You'll need the exploded block with your new attribute modifications before you'll be able to use the command. Let's review the ATTREDEF command sequence:

```
Command: attredef
Name of Block you wish to redefine:
Enter the name of the block you need to redefine.
Select objects for new Block...
```

Select the objects, including attributes, that comprise the updated block. Remember, that attribute can be important.

```
Select objects: Other corner: 13 found
Select objects:
Insertion base point of new Block:
```

**Figure 11:** Edit
Attributes dialog box.

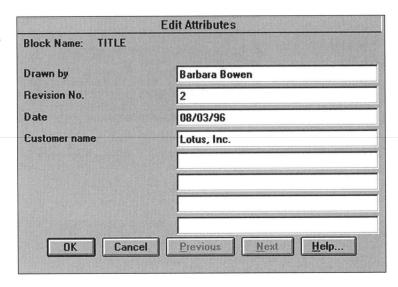

Be sure that you are using the same insertion point as you did previously. All of your existing blocks should update using the attribute modifications. If you've added an attribute to the block, you'll notice that AutoCAD uses the default value you selected. If that isn't desirable, you can edit them individually using DDATTE.

Take the extra time to add attributes to some of your library symbols, and, in the long run, you'll find yourself saving time and preventing excess work .

# Made to Order Menus

AutoCAD's open architecture has always been one of its strong points. The ability to easily customize the drawing environment to suit your individual needs enables you to create a drawing editor that feels like your favorite arm chair. You can surround yourself with your favorite AutoCAD commands, create macros to avoid those extra tedious steps, and save yourself hours of unnecessary work.

Prior to Release 13, the AutoCAD menus consisted of two files: *acad.mnx* and *acad.mnu*. The *.mnu* file was an ASCII text file written by Autodesk programmers (perhaps with additions from yourself). The *.mnx* file was simply a compiled version of the same menu. In the interest of our valuable time, AutoCAD reads only the *.mnx* file, which makes reading much faster. If you edit the *.mnu* file, AutoCAD automatically recompiles the file to create a new *.mnx*.

Over the years, you may have altered, made additions to, or created your own ACAD menu file from scratch. Whatever the case, you probably began to dread the new releases of AutoCAD for one very good reason: you were forced to update your precious custom menus. AutoCAD Release 13 implemented a great new tool referred to as Partial Menu Loading that lets you sandwich your existing custom menus between the pull-down menus. This new procedure requires just one minor modification to your existing menu, which we'll cover later.

The menu file extensions for AutoCAD are:

```
.mnu template file
.mns source file
.mnc compiled source file
.mnr resource file
```

as well as

```
.mnl AutoLISP menu file
.mnd menu definition file
```

The *.mnu* file is referred to as the template file. It is within this ASCII text file that the menu is programmed. If you want to add to or modify the ACAD menu, you begin here. The .mnu file closely resembles the menu structures of the past. Items you want to save forever (like your favorite custom toolbars) should be saved within the *.mnu* file; these specifications hold true for the DOS version, as well.

The *.mns* file is also ASCII and looks quite similar to the *.mnu* file, sans formatting or comment sections. In reality, this file is a cleaner version of the *.mnu* file. Any changes that occur to your toolbar or menus from within the drawing editor are saved to the *.mns* file.

The *.mnc* file is similar to the *.mnx* file of the past from DOS. It's a compiled version of the *.mns* file; in fact, AutoCAD loads and uses only compiled binary menu files. To do otherwise causes AutoCAD's menus to perform very slowly.

The *.mnr* file is a binary file that contains the bitmaps for your icons. As you modify a button using the icon editor in AutoCAD, this file is updated.

The *.mnl* file, which hasn't changed from the Release 12 version, contains any LISP routines that go along with your menu. It is loaded into memory when a menu file with the same name is loaded.

The *.mnd* file is also the same as in Release 12. These menu

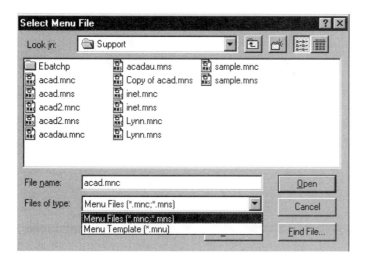

files contain macros for quick menu customization. An auxiliary program called mc.exe (sample directory) creates a usable menu file out of an .mnd file.

This explanation may have cleared up some of the new-menu fog, but there's much more to this structure. Examining the way AutoCAD deals with the different menu types might clear the way even further.

Let's open AutoCAD. As you bring up the drawing editor, AutoCAD searches for a menu. The file it searches for is *acad.mnc.* If it can't find *acad.mnc,* it will search for *acad.mns.* If found, it will compile it and load the newly created *acad.mnc.*

You may also indicate to AutoCAD that you'd like it to load a *.mnu* file. Should you choose to do this, AutoCAD will display a dialog box warning that you are about to lose your custom toolbars if you continue. All of your custom toolbars are saved to the *.mns* file. Be sure to heed this warning if you've spent a sub-stantial amount of time creating some nifty toolbars. On the other hand, should you mess up your desktop completely, every-thing will remain safe and sound in the *acad.mnu* file. Loading the *acad.mnu* file will restore your original desktop settings.

But where did your new customized toolbars go? They were deleted along with the *.mns* file. Before you delete the , be sure to copy your new toolbars to the *.mnu.* We'll address this task later in the article.

Let's look at the inner workings of the *.mnu* (and *.mns*) file. Veteran menu customizers will notice the name of the ***ICON section was changed to ***IMAGE in Release 13. The programming syntax is the same, but the name has been changed. Your old menus will still work, but I suggest you begin to make the transition for future releases of AutoCAD. AutoCAD Release 13 added four new sections to the Windows menus:

***MENUGROUP
***TOOLBARS
***HELPSTRINGS
***ACCELERATORS

The MENUGROUP section is essential for partial menu loading. This new MENUGROUP section works with the new name tag assignments, as well. Each menu file has its own group name, and each menu item can have its own individual name tag. This setup allows you to call back this menu item from other parts of your menu.

Imagine a lengthy menu item you'd like to assign to an accelerator key. Rather then repeat the lengthy macro, you can call it via its name. Any time you think you'll want to refer back to a particular menu item, assign a name tag. For a more advanced example, let's gray-out or deactivate a menu item. Previous releases would ask for a menu position when graying out (menucmd "P1.2=~"). What if someone rearranged the menu? Now the wrong menu item is deactivated. Using name tags, you can call to it using its name. AutoCAD will find this name tag, which is located in the menu. All the name tags in the ACAD menu begin with "ID_", such as "ID_LIST". You don't have to follow this syntax when creating name tags—you can call your name tags "Fred" and "Ethel" and get the same results. Typically, you create a name tag that relates to the menu item. The Menugroup name for the ACAD menu is "ACAD."

The TOOLBARS section contains the tool palettes. This section doesn't need to be hard-coded from within the *acad.mnu* because it can be created using the Toolbar option in the View pull-down menu. This option lets you visually customize a tool palette, which is much easier than manually programming it.

Helpstrings are those comments that appear in the lower left-hand corner of the drawing editor along the status line. A helpstring tells you what a menu item or tool button would do if selected. As you move your cursor over the items on any of the ACAD pull-down menus, you'll notice these helpstrings pop up. The proper syntax for the Helpstrings section is a name tag followed by the helpstring, such as ID_Circle [This command is used to draw a circle].

If you want to preserve toolbars indefinitely, place them in the *acad.mnu* file. You'll have to get them from the *acad.mns* file, which is accomplished by opening the *acad.mns* file (using WRITE will do fine), and searching for the TOOLBARS section. Let's say you have created a new toolbar called FAVORITES. Within this toolbar palette, you've placed four of your favorite commands: SAVE, LINE, ERASE, and UNDO. You will search for FAVORITES under the TOOLBARS section of the *acad.mns* file (it should be at the tail end of the TOOLBARS section).

Copy this section of *acad.mns* to the clipboard and open the *acad.mnu* file. Find the TOOLBARS section and paste your toolbar into the menu.

If you've modified the HELPSTRINGS section, you'll need to find the helpstring attached to the button and take it along, as well. Simply go to the HELPSTRINGS section and cut and paste the appropriate ones. For example, let's say you changed the Erase button to read "Corrects Lynn's Mistakes," you will see that AutoCAD increments the name tag from "ID_ERASE_0" to "ID_ERASE_1." Search for this name tag in the HELPSTRINGS section. It will look something like:

```
***HELPSTRINGS
ID_ERASE_1  [Corrects Lynn's Mistakes]
```

After saving this information to the *.mnu* file (which isn't as painful as it sounds), you've preserved your precious toolbar forever.

I'm going to add another sneaky method of saving your toolbars to the *.mnu* file ... how about copying the *.mns* file over the *.mnu* file? There's technically nothing wrong with that and it's much easier then the tedious task of transferring the individual bits of information. I'd make sure I save a clean copy of the *.mnu* file somewhere else for safe keeping (just in case).

AutoCAD Release 13 also added the ability to assign accelerator keys or hot keys. You can assign AutoCAD commands to any unused function keys (F3, F4, F11, F12) and to key combinations, such as <Shift+A>. These new accelerators are simple and look like this:

```
***ACCELERATORS
["F3"]'ZOOM;2x
["F4"]'ZOOM;.8x
[Control+"C"]^C
[Shift+"A"]^C^CArc
[Shift+Control+"O"]+
^C^Coffset
ID_ERASE [Shift+"E"]
```

Function keys are double quoted. You can use <Ctrl>, <Shift>, or both in conjunction with a standard alphanumeric key. If you're mapping an accelerator to a name tag, the name tag needs to come first (see previous example). These keys are also available:

```
<Home>
<End>
<Insert>
<Delete>
```

You are not permitted to use <Alt> because it is used for existing mnemonics. A mnemonic key is one that, when combined with <Alt>, activates a particular menu item. For example, <Alt+F> pulls down the File menu. But be careful not to assign an accelerator key to an existing control-key combination, such as <Ctrl+E>.

You DOS veterans may have noticed that <Ctrl+C> in the Windows version does a COPYCLIP rather than a cancel. You can restore CANCEL by modifying the Accelerator keys in the acad or *acadfull.mnu* files, as discussed previously. But, if you have corrected this problem by selecting the AutoCAD Classic option in the Preferences dialog box, you have turned off all of your accelerator keys. To enable your accelerator keys, you'll need to return the Keystrokes section back to Menu File. If you have no  idea what I'm talking about, you've probably already adjusted to using <Esc> as a cancel.

You might create a sample menu that looks like the one in Listing 1. The ampersand (&) denotes the mnemonic key.

After creating your own menu, you can go into the MENU-LOAD command and sandwich your menu into the existing base menu (ACAD). You can also use MENULOAD to remove or add individual pull downs to the base menu. The only menu sections that are loaded with MENULOAD are the pull downs, toolbars, and helpstrings. The accelerators are only accessible from the base menu.

I hope this overview of the AutoCAD menu structure will get you started on the road to creating an AutoCAD environment that fits your needs. Take advantage of AutoCAD's simple programming interface and make it the arm chair of your dreams!

# Customized Toolbars

AutoCAD Release 13 marked the beginning of a true separation between the Windows and DOS platforms. Several of the new features available on Windows are either unavailable in DOS or seriously wounded. The drawing editor is just one of the many areas where these two versions of AutoCAD differ. Because of these differences, a veteran DOS user can feel very uncomfortable working in AutoCAD for Windows or vice versa.

The first obvious differences are the new Windows toolbars. Although a bit overwhelming at first, the toolbars can become your best friend. Never has it been easier to create and modify the user interface, which means you can take your favorite commands and easily place them in your own customized toolbar.

Before we get started with toolbar customization, let's cover some basic syntax. A toolbar is made up of several tools; the pictures on the tools are called icons. A toolbar with many tools is often referred to as a palette, which can be docked (fixed) along the top or sides of the drawing editor, or left floating on the screen.

You can use the Tools pull-down menu to select the Customize Toolbars option, which will take you to the Toolbar dialog box or TBCONFIG command, as shown in Figure 1. You can

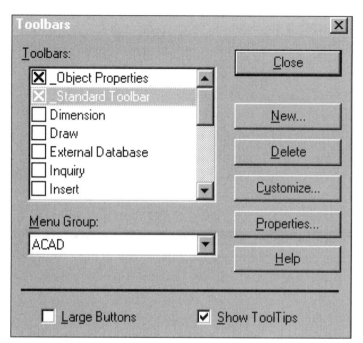

**Figure 1:** Use the TBCONFIG command to customize your toolbar.

also get to this dialog box by right-clicking on any existing tool. Within the dialog box is a listing of existing toolbars:

• **Close:** closes the dialog box.

• **New:** creates a new toolbar using a name of your choosing.

• **Delete:** removes existing toolbars (Be careful with this one).

• **Customize:** creates a new toolbar, AutoCAD selects the name

• **Properties:** used to rename, or change the helpstrings of existing toolbars (see Figure 2).

• **Large Buttons:** displays the 32 x 32 pixels tool size (rather then the 16 x 16). Large buttons are great for those with bad eyesight or very high resolution graphics cards.

• **Show Tooltips:** displays the command associated with a tool.

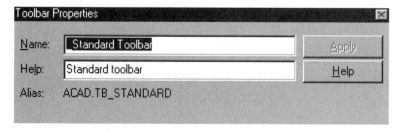

**Figure 2:** Properties can be used to rename, or change helpstrings of existing toolbars.

## Creating a Toolbar

Let's begin by creating a new toolbar. Pick the New option and create a toolbar we will call Favorite. This will create a small empty toolbar titled Favorite. Position the toolbar so it's easily accessible for customizing.

Now we want to add tools to our toolbar, and there are two methods for doing this. One way is to select the Customize option from the dialog box. This will place you in Toolbar Customization mode, as shown in Figure 3.

Selecting a category will display a palette of tools. Pick and drag this tool to your new toolbar. You may select as many tools from as many different categories as you like. Tools with a small black triangle in the lower lefthand corner contain fly-outs (many tools available from one). To add completely blank tools or blank fly-outs, select the Custom toolbar category, which contains two empty tools (one is a fly-out). Empty tools are useful if you plan to create a tool such as library symbols from scratch. Add several tools to your new toolbar.

Note that the tooltips don't display on the icons, which makes it difficult to tell which tool you're dragging until you've placed it in the toolbar. If you find you've picked the wrong tool, just drag it off the toolbar into space and it will disappear (for this to occur you must be in Toolbar Customization mode).

You may also add tools to your new toolbar by using the

**Figure 3:** To add tools to your toolbars, choose the customize option, which places you in toolbar customization mode.

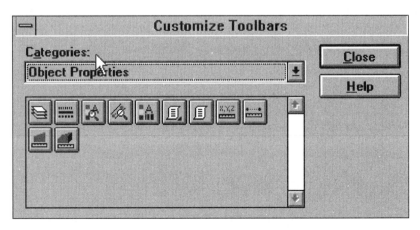

216

existing toolbars. Dragging and dropping will simply move the tools from one palette to another. Holding down the Control key while you're dragging will place a copy of the desired tool in the new toolbar (which is probably the approach you'd want to take). Using existing tools allows you to see the tooltip prior to dragging them to your new toolbar, which eliminates the possibility of selecting an incorrect tool.

While in Toolbar Customization mode, you can rearrange or add spaces between your tools. Separating the tools with spaces makes them easier to select and less confusing. Drag the tools to the right and left edge of the tool without going past the middle of the tool. To reposition the tools in your toolbar, drag the tool to the new location. You must go more than halfway across the existing tool in the desired location.

## Modifying the Toolbar Commands

AutoCAD Release 13 also provided easy access to the commands your tools execute. Perhaps you'd like your Text tool to set your current layer to Text before creating any text. If you choose to create a toolbar with some library symbols, you'll need to program the tools to insert the blocks. You can easily modify or completely change a tool's function inside AutoCAD (this does require a little MENU customization knowledge).

While in Toolbar Customization mode, right-click on the tool you want to modify. This will take you to the Button Properties dialog box, as shown in Figure 4.

In this dialog box you can control the following:

- The tooltip (Name)—erase.
- The helpstring (Help)—removes objects from a drawing.
- The command(s) executed when the tool is selected (Macro)—"^C^C_erase.
- The Button icon.

If you want the tooltip or helpstring to read something different, replace the existing text. The macros can also be easily modified to suit your needs. Button macros are created the

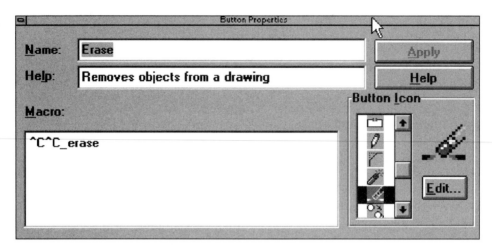

**Figure 4:** The button properties dialog box lets you modify a specific tool.

same way menu macros are. AutoCAD Release 12 had it's own button syntax that wasn't consistent with it's menus—this is much nicer. Here is a quick menu customization review:

```
^C cancel
; enter
\ pause for user input
```

The Buttons Properties dialog box also allows you to change icons. You can choose from the existing list or create your own. The tool icons may be created externally inside a bitmap creating program (like paint) or internally within AutoCAD. Creating these files externally requires following some simple rules. Create a bitmap 16x16 pixels and another 32x32 (for large buttons). Save the two files with a .BMP extension.

To create an icon within AutoCAD, select <Edit> from the Button Properties dialog box. This will take you to the Button Editor, shown in Figure 5.

The button editor displays a thumbnail sketch of the icon in the upper left corner (actual size) and a larger view for editing. If you prefer working with a pixel grid displayed on the icon, you can do so by toggling the Grid option on. To erase the existing icon completely, pick <Clear>. To open an existing BMP file, select Open. The color palette is displayed on the right side of the button editor. Select a color, and choose from the following drawing tools:

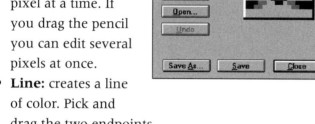

**Figure 5:** The button editor lets you create an icon inside Auto-CAD.

- **Pencil:** edits one pixel at a time. If you drag the pencil you can edit several pixels at once.
- **Line:** creates a line of color. Pick and drag the two endpoints.
- **Circle:** pick the radius and drag to set the radius.
- **Erase:** sets the color to white and erases existing pixels.

The Undo option will undo the last edit function.

After creating your icon, save your creation. The Save option will store the icon under a predetermined icon number/name. The Saveas option allows you to specify the icon name. Close to exit the Button editor.

Modifying the icons in AutoCAD Release 12 was a serious investment in time. Release 13 streamlined this process and made it incredibly easy.

To save any icon or Button Properties changes you must pick the Apply option. This will write back to the *acad.mns* and the *acad.mnr* files (which may take a few seconds to recompile).

It should be noted that these custom toolbars are saved only in the *acad.mns* file and not the mnu. should you choose to save them permanently you will need to transfer your custom toolbar from the ***TOOLBAR section of the *mns* to the same section located in the *mnu* file. See the last chapter for further instruction on this subject.

Modifying and creating new toolbars is simple and can shave hours off your design time. Set your toolbars up exactly the way you think they should be. If you never use a command in a toolbar, get rid of it! Simplify your drawing editor by keeping only those tools visible that you use (you can always put them back later).

# Limitless Linetypes

inetypes are an integral part of nearly all CAD applications. Two serious linetype restrictions were removed in AutoCAD Release 13. AutoCAD has always limited us to one linetype scale factor for all of our linetypes. This was a frustrating restriction but we adjusted accordingly by creating our own. The various linetypes of the past were also limiting in that they were expressed only as a simple combination of lines, spaces, and dots. Release 13 removed these restrictions, enabling multiple linetype scale factors for each drawing. Customization also became a little easier in Release 13, where linetypes permit the addition of text strings or shapes to linetypes. To create simple linetypes, we can use the **linetype** command. Simple linetypes are made up of dashes, spaces, and dots only. Issue the linetype command:

```
Command: LINETYPE
?/Create/Load/Set: C
Name of linetype to create: sample
```

At this point, AutoCAD will display the Create or Append Linetype File dialog box. Let's create our own linetype file of

Test. The following will open a file called TEST.LIN and ready it for storing information:

```
Descriptive text: first sample linetype
Enter pattern (on next line)
A,
```

All linetype pattern definitions begin with A, which signifies the pattern alignment. AutoCAD only supports A-type alignment, which ensures that all lines and arcs start and end with a dash. Because no options are available at this point, AutoCAD included A so we can't make a mistake. To define the rest of a basic linetype definition:

```
a positive number = a vector
a negative number = a space
0 = a dot.
```

AutoCAD uses a comma as a delimiter. 1.5,-.25,0,-.25 would be equal to a vector 1.5 units long, a space (gap) of .25, a dot, and another space of .25. This definition could be used to define an entire linetype. Add these values to our definition:

```
A,1.5,-.25,0,-.25
```

After creating the linetype, we need to load it into our drawing. While we're still in the **linetype** command, let's load this linetype:

```
Linetype(s) to load: SAMPLE
```

Find the TEST.LIN file from the file dialog box. After loading the linetype, we'll set this to be the current linetype.

```
?/Create/Load/Set: S
New object linetype (or ?): SAMPLE
```

Any new objects you draw should display our new linetype. If for some reason you do not see lines and dots on new objects, you may need to increase or decrease your ltscale factor.

The linetypes that come with AutoCAD are stored in a file called ACAD.LIN (the Support subdirectory). Feel free to open up this file and look at the various linetype definitions. You'll see no surprises.

Complex linetypes fulfill a longtime need, which many of us have resorted to third-party packages to satisfy. We'll create a simple linetype with the text "Fence" built into it. It should visually resemble Figure 1.

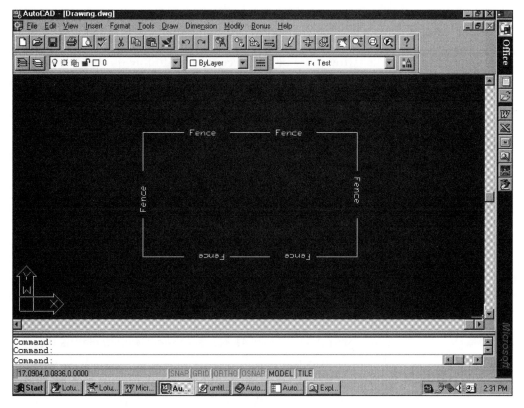

**Figure 1:** A simple linetype with text.

Complex linetypes cannot be constructed internally within the linetype command. Instead, we'll need to use an external text editor. If you're on the Windows platform, you can use Write or Notepad. DOS users can shell out to Edit or your favorite text editor. Open the TEST.LIN file we've already started. You'll see our original linetype definition (Sample) already listed within. Notice that our linetype definition consists of two

223

lines. The first line starts with an asterisk and contains the name of the linetype followed by an optional description (maximum of 47 characters). The second line of code contains the actual coded definition, which must always begin with A. AutoCAD will reject any other character placed in the alignment field.

We're going to name our new linetype Fence. The Fence linetype consists simply of a vector, the word Fence, followed by another vector. We're going to need to include some extra information to create our complex linetype. Let's review what we'll need:

- **Text:** the text string we want to include within our linetype. This string must be enclosed within double quotes. In our case, it will be the word "Fence."

- **Text style:** the text style we want AutoCAD to use to display the text. We'll use the Standard text style since all drawings have this text style included within. Be aware that this must be an existing text style, and not a font. The text style is not enclosed within double quotes.

- **Text height:** the text height when the linetype scale factor is set to 1. As the ltscale factor is modified, so is the text height. For example, if we set the text height to .2 and the ltscale factor is set to 3, the total text height will be .6. We'll set our height to .2. This factor is often hit and miss and must be tried at several values to get the desired result. We'll set our text height to .2 by including the phrase S=.2. (S stands for scale factor.) The *AutoCAD Customization Manual* claims that this value is actually a multiplier of the text style height; however, this doesn't seem to be the case. This value appears to be absolute, regardless of the style setting for text height. So don't think of this value as a scale factor—think of it as a text height.

- **Rotation angle:** controls the rotation angle for the text string. If you want the text to follow the same angle as the object you're drawing you'll set this value to 0. Any angle is acceptable. We can use two modifiers for setting the angle—A for absolute rotation and R for relative rotation. If we set

"A=0" we would be forcing the text to remain at 0 degrees regardless of the direction of the object drawn. "R=0" would force a rotation angle of 0 relative or tangential to the direction of the object drawn. We'll use R=0.

- **x and y displacement:** controls the displacement of the text from the last vector. If we wanted to place the word Fence slightly above the last vector, we might set the *y* position to .1. To center the text, we will need to set the *y* to a negative number, pulling the text downward. We will set the text displacement to *y* =-.1. If you want to modify the *x* displacement, you can, although it's usually not necessary. We'll leave *x* at 0.

Any value you want to assume to be 0, need not be entered. We'll be including *x* and *r* (though they have values of 0) only for practice. Any lines of code starting with a semicolon will be ignored if you want to make comments. Now we're ready to create our Linetype. Add this to the TEST.LIN file:

```
*Fence, sample complex linetype
A,1.5,-.25,["Fence", Standard,S=.2,R=0,X=0, Y=-.1],-1.5
```

A stands for alignment, 1.5 draws a 1.5 unit vector, -.25 creates a .25 space, and -1.5 allows enough space from the beginning of the string "Fence" to the next vector—the reason this value is so big.

Save this file and reenter the linetype command. Load and set the new linetype. As you draw new objects, you should see the newly created complex linetype.

You can also use shape files within your custom linetype file. Remember how to create shape files? Unlike blocks, shape files are difficult and cumbersome to create. Years ago, AutoCAD operators who were unhappy with the existing text fonts (there were only four) were forced to learn the ancient art of creating shape files to make their own text fonts. Some of those people who mastered the art went on to create multiple fonts and sell them to the AutoCAD masses. Even today, with the vast variety of fonts provided with AutoCAD software, many of you still use third-party fonts in your drawings.

Shape files are hard-coded ASCII text files. Using a combination of pen up/down, vector lengths, and angles, you explain to AutoCAD how to draw your shape. This explanation process is much more difficult than it appears. The *Customization Manual* includes explicit instructions on how to create shape files, if you feel up to the task. In the early days of AutoCAD, shape files were often used in place of blocks in a drawing. Shape files were believed to be faster and more compact files. Working on an 8088 processor, a CAD user would do anything to save time. Years ago, a package called AutoShapes let you create shape files by drawing the desired figure within AutoCAD. AutoShapes would convert your drawing into a shape file and do all the laborious work for you. It would have been nice if the makers of this product reinvented their wheel and reintroduced this product.

Should you find yourself with an existing shape file you want to place within a complex linetype, you'll notice only a slight difference between the complex linetype with text. You'll need to know the names of the shape and the compiled shape file (extension of .SHX).

If you had a shape file called RR that existed within a shape file called DEMO.SHX, your linetype may look like this:

```
*Railroad, sample linetype with a shape file
A,1.5,-.25,[RR, demo.shx,S=.5,A=0,X=0, Y=-.1],-1.0
```

AutoCAD knows RR is a shape file rather than text because it's not double quoted.

As was mentioned earlier, AutoCAD now provides the ability to have multiple linetype scale factors per drawing. Previously, we had the ltscale command, which controlled the linetype scale factor for the entire drawing. We often had to create multiple linetypes with varying vector lengths to get the desired effect. Now a new system variable, the Current Entity Linetype Scale (celtscale), can control the ltscale factor for individual entities. Set this value before you draw the intended objects. This value can be set in the Ddemodes dialog box (Data pull-down menu—Object Creation option). If you've already drawn some objects and want to change their ltscale factor, use the **ddchprop**, **chprop**, **change**, or **ddmodify** commands.

Nearly all CAD applications use linetypes in their drawings. These new improvements should speed up drawing time and eliminate the Band-Aids we've used in the past.

# Setting Up Your Files Structure with Preferences

The Preferences dialog box came into its own in Auto-CAD R13. It was filled with many key variables and settings, and users could explore and modify the five tabs to improve their productivity. Now, Autodesk has really packed a punch into the Preferences dialog box with R14. There are definitely some need-to-know features in here, but I am only going to cover file structures in this section.

The Preferences dialog box can be accessed in five different ways: key in the incredibly long command (the word PREFER-ENCES—ugh!); use the new alias of PR; use the old CONFIG command; select it from the Tools pull-down menu (as in R13); or—my personal favorite—take advantage of the new, improved user interface by right-clicking over the command prompt area and selecting it from the cursor menu. Any one of these above methods will bring up the new, improved Preferences dialog box, as shown in Figure 1.

On opening the Preferences dialog, users will see that it has been completely revamped. It's now broken into eight sections: Files, Performance, Compatibility, General, Display, Pointer, Printer, and Profiles.

228

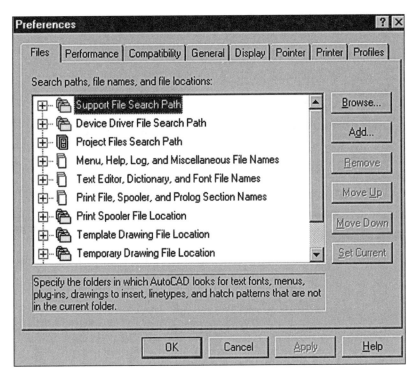

**Figure 1:** The information-packed Preferences dialog box can be accessed in several ways in R14.

## Tapping Into the Files Tab Riches

Now it's easier than ever to set up the path structure that Auto-CAD uses for file searching. Within the Files tab, you can specify the directories (in Windows terminology, the folders) where AutoCAD looks to find things, such as text fonts, linetypes, menus, and files you choose to insert. If these paths are properly set, your AutoCAD drawing days will be bright and happy. If not, you'll definitely have a rough time trying to convince AutoCAD to find any external files and information.

The method for setting these search paths is simple. Select the directory or file from the list. This list displays the directories AutoCAD is currently using to search. To add another directory, pick Add from the right side of the dialog box. This action will open a placeholder for the new directory, as shown in Figure 2.

You can key in the path and name of the directory you wish to add to the search list or click the Browse button to manually

**Figure 2:** Adding a
directory to the
Support File Search
Path is easy. Just
click Add and enter
the new information.

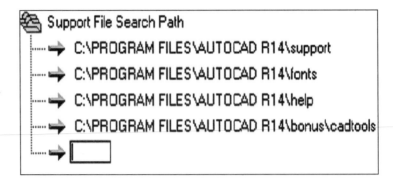

select the directory. I recommend the latter to ensure there are
no typing errors.

You'll also find that you can use the Remove button to
delete a directory from the search path. AutoCAD searches the
paths in the order in which they are displayed in the Preferences dialog box. The Move Up and Move Down buttons can
be used to control the search-path priority. Using Figure 2 as
an example, I could decide that I want AutoCAD to search the
bonus\cadtools directory before any other directory. I can
select this directory and use the Move Up key to move it to the
first position.

Briefly, I'll cover the different files and directories where
users can add search paths. You'll see that there are many
different options within the Files tab.

## Support Files

These files consist of hatch patterns, linetypes, and files you
want to insert. It's not uncommon for power users to include
the directory within the search path where their library symbols
can be found.

## Device Driver Files

These files contain the path that AutoCAD searches for ADI dri-
vers to support digitizers, printers, or video display.

## Project Files

These files represent one of the most powerful changes to the Preferences dialog box. Now, users are able to set up different search paths for external references for different projects.

For example, you can be working on two different projects: one of a hospital and one of an office building. You can use distinctly different external reference files for the two projects, and use this tab to set up two different project folders, as shown in Figure 3. One folder can contain the directories to reference for the hospital project; one the directories to use for the office project.

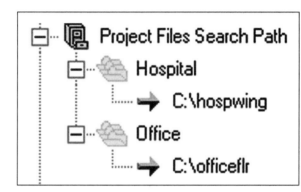

**Figure 3:** Project Files, such as those shared with concurrent-engineering team members, can be specified in the Project Files Search Path.

Tell AutoCAD which project you're using by setting it to be current with the Set Current button on the right of the dialog. The definitions of the project search paths are stored in AutoCAD's global settings, but which Project Path is attached to a drawing (if any) is stored in the **projectname** system variable. This is saved with the drawing.

You'll also find this feature valuable if you're practicing concurrent engineering. If several of your coworkers are referencing the same group of files, you may need to specify on which server directory these files are located. This setting can vary from project to project.

## Menu, Help, Log, and Miscellaneous File Names

You'll notice this section contains the names of specific files for AutoCAD to use rather than directories.

I've received several emails from users wondering where these filenames are stored in R14, so here they are!

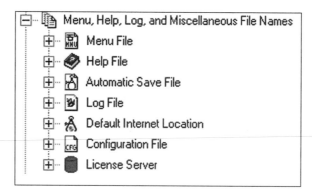

**Figure 4:** The Menu, Help, Log and Miscellaneous File Names search path contains many useful settings.

This section contains several useful settings, as shown in Figure 4, including:

- **Menu File.** The default menu file to use. The default is *acad*.
- **Help File.** The default help file—set to *acad.hlp*.
- **Automatic Save File.** The name of the file that defaults to *auto.sv$*. If you have your automatic saving time set to a reasonable value, AutoCAD will save your drawing as you go, whether you remember to do it manually or not. AutoCAD is doing so under the drawing name of *auto.sv$*. As we all know, this doesn't look like a drawing file at all because of the extension. I prefer to change this file to have a DWG extension. Then, if you find yourself losing a great deal of drawing information for some reason (AutoCAD hanging for example), you can salvage this file for use. If you leave the filename at *auto.sv$*, you'll need to rename it to a DWG extension before you'll be able to open it. This necessity can be very confusing for new AutoCAD users. This setting can also be set with the **savefile** system variable.
- **Log File.** The name of the Log File that gets created when you select the Maintain a Log File option in the General tab (default *acad.log*). This records the text information of the AutoCAD text window. This name can also be set in the **logfilename** system variable.
- **Default Internet Location.** The Default Internet Location (which isn't a filename at all) defaults to *www.autodesk.com/acaduser*. This Web site is used when you select the

Connect to Internet option on the Help menu, and it's also saved in the **inetlocation** system variable.

- **Configuration File.** The Configuration File (*acad14.cfg*) is a read-only file that cannot be changed from within this dialog. If you are using the Autodesk License Manager, you'll also find the location of the network server here.

## Text Editor, Dictionary, and Font File Names

The following settings, as shown in Figure 5, are contained within this section:

- **Text Editor Application.** This setting is the name of the default text editor used by MTEXT (typically set to internal). You probably aren't going to want to change this value. You can also use the **mtexted** system variable.
- **Main Dictionary.** You want to use this setting for spell check (there are several to choose from). This information is also saved in the **dctmain** system variable.
- **Custom Dictionary File.** This setting is the name of your custom dictionary file, if you're using one. This value is stored in the **dctcust** system variable.
- **Alternate Font File.** Use this setting when AutoCAD can't find a particular text font (the **fontalt** system variable) as it pulls up a drawing. This usually happens when you get drawings from other people.
- **Font Mapping File.** This setting is improperly documented in the Help function as well as in the dialog box (tell me no!).

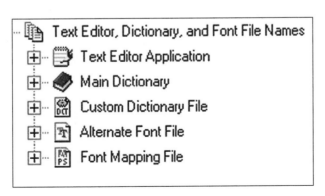

**Figure 5:** The Text Editor Dictionary and Font File Names settings.

233

Actually, this file contains font substitutions you may choose to use for time-saving purposes or to substitute for known missing fonts. If your drawing contains many true type fonts and you feel they are slowing you down, you can map them to simpler fonts, such as TXT, until you plot. This style can also be set with the **fontmap** system variable.

## Print File, Spooler, and Prolog Section Names

This section is used for files related to printing/plotting.

- **Print File Names.** This file is used to set the name of the default plot file. Setting this value to "." will use the name of the current drawing file for the plot file. You'll notice the dot is the default (which looks kind of strange).
- **Print Spool Executable.** This file would contain the name of your print spooling application if you had one configured.
- **PostScript Prolog Section Name.** This file applies to those of you who create customized prolog sections in the *acad.psf* file (Are there many of you who do that?). The system variable **psprolog** can also be used to set this one.

## Printer Spooler File Location

This option is used to set the path for print spool files.

## Template Drawing File Location

This section is used to tell AutoCAD where your Template files are located (DWT). Template files are the R14 replacement for prototype drawings. The new Start Up Wizard uses this search path to find the template files it displays.

## Temporary Drawing File Location

This is the location that AutoCAD uses to store temporary files—more specifically, those related to your drawing file. Now that we have Temporary External Reference files, we need

to distinguish the difference. By default, they go to the
*Windows\Temp* directory.

## Temporary External Reference File Location

New to R14 is the ability to copy a demand-loaded external
reference. This copy will reside in the location assigned here.
This also defaults to the *Windows\Temp* directory.

## Texture Maps Search Path

Last but not least, this contains the directories AutoCAD will
search for rendering texture maps.

# Cool System Variables
## (a.k.a. SETVARs)

To be a true AutoCAD wizard, you have to know a few incredibly cool system variables. Veteran AutoCAD users will throw out system variable names right and left just to impress the socks off the new kid on the block. Sometimes it sounds as though they're speaking a foreign CAD language! I'm going to expose you to some of the extra cool system variables so you, too, can cavort with the CAD elders.

Why do the CAD elders hold on to their SETVAR knowledge? Because they know the importance of unlocking the system variable doors to enhanced productivity. Most of the system variables can be accessed through dialog boxes or alternate commands—but some of them cannot—which means, if you don't know what it is or does, you won't be able to take advantage of its power. System variables are also great assets to menu macros (or toolbars). You can't tell a menu macro to pick a check box on a dialog box—you have to know the name of the system variable.

We won't be covering all the system variables—just a few choice ones. We'll cover a few of the more powerful (and popular) SETVARs that you might choose to strategically place in your everyday CAD life.

SETVARs have ugly technical names. Because of this, many users have run from them thinking they're too advanced to understand or use. Well, SETVARs are not difficult, they just look that way. So hold on!

System variables can be saved in a variety of places, and where they're saved can be very important. If a system variable is saved in the configuration file, then this setting will affect all of your drawings. If the system variable is saved in the drawing file, it will only affect future revisions of the same drawing. If you would like these system variables to affect all new drawings, you will need to change the setting within your various template files. Some system variables are not saved at all—they are valid only for the current drawing session and will resort back to their default value the next time you open the drawing.

Here is a selection of system variables in alphabetical order:

## Attdia

**Advantage:** Attributes become more user friendly.
**Function:** When set to a value of 1, an attribute dialog box will display instead of the command prompt interface.
**Default:** 0 (Off-No dialog box)
**Saved in:** Drawing file.

## Attreq

**Advantage:** Speeds up the process of inserting blocks with attributes.
**Function:** When set to 0, AutoCAD assigns the default attribute value to all attributes and suppresses the attribute prompts. If you're in a hurry and don't have time to enter attribute information, you can set attreq to 0, turn the attribute display off (ATTDISP command), and enter the attribute values at a later time.
**Default:** 1 (on)
**Saved in:** Drawing file

## Clayer

**Advantage:** A fast method of setting a new current layer (transparently).

**Function:** If you want to quickly change to a new current layer from within a command, you can execute the CLAYER command and key in the desired layer command. If you're a dialog box junkie, you won't care for this function. If you create layers with incredibly long names, you won't care for it either. If, however, you like to key in commands, this method is a speedy way of changing layers. Better yet, you can include this command in your menu and toolbar macros to ensure you're on the correct layer before executing certain commands. The Layer drop-down list is a great method of changing current layers, but can't be executed transparently.

**Default:** current layer name

**Saved in:** Drawing file

**Figure 1:** Dispsilh set to 1.

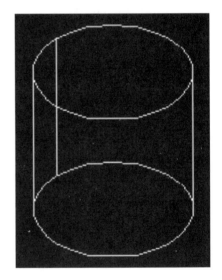

## Dispsilh (Release 13 and up)

**Advantage:** Improves 3D viewing with little decrease in speed.

**Function:** When set to 1, AutoCAD displays the silhouette curves of 3D objects (in wire-frame mode). Combining this setting with a low value for ISOLINES permits quick viewing with reasonable drawing detail. Imagine facing a wall, holding an object, and shining a flashlight on the object. The silhouette (the outline of the shadow) would shine on the wall. This silhouette is similar to the one **dispsilh** controls.

**Default:** 0 (off)

**Saved in:** Drawing file

# Expert

**Advantage:** Turns off those annoying extra prompts. Not recommended for beginners (hence the name, **expert**).

**Function:** Controls the issuance of certain prompts provided to ensure that the user doesn't make a mistake. If you're a well-versed AutoCAD user, you probably don't need to see these same prompts over and over. Several values of **expert** control several different types of prompts.

1. Suppresses two all-familiar prompts: "About to regen, proceed?" (caused when REGENAUTO is turned off) and "Really want to turn the current layer off?"
2. Also suppresses "Block already defined. Redefine it?" (BLOCK command). **Expert** set to 2 is also supposed to suppress the prompt "A drawing with this name already exists. Overwrite it?" (SAVE, SAVEAS, or WBLOCK command) but doesn't hold true in Release 13.
3. In addition to 1 and 2, a value of 3 suppresses prompts issued by the LINETYPE command should you try to load previously loaded linetypes or create duplicate linetype names within the same file.
4. In addition to all of the previous values, a value of 4 suppresses those warning prompts when you try to save a UCS or VPORT with a previously defined name.
5. In addition to all of the previous values, this one suppresses those warning prompts when you try to save a dimension style with a previously defined name.

Suppressing any or all of these prompts simply means that AutoCAD will assume you know what you're doing and accept a value of Yes, which means "Yes, I want to turn off my current layer," "Yes, I want to reload this linetype," and so on. The Super AutoCAD operator might choose to live dangerously by selecting an **expert** value of 5.

**Default:** 0 (off) Does this mean AutoCAD's inferring we're not all experts?

**Saved in:** Not saved (valid for drawing sessions only)

**Figure 2:** Facetres set to .5.

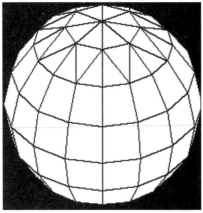

**Figure 3:** Facetres set to 2.

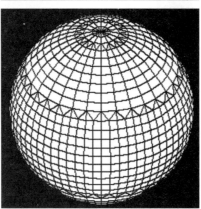

# Facetres (Release 13 and up)

**Advantage:** Very useful in improving the display of 3D shading and hidden line removal. Can also affect rendering.

**Function:** Controls the resolution of the various facets that appear while hiding, shading, and rendering. Acceptable values range from .01 to 10. Even a value of 2 can produce a nicely faceted object. Any value less than 0.5 starts to dramatically decrease the smoothness of any solid objects. The higher the value of facetres, the slower you'll find hiding, shading, and rendering and obviously the opposite is true as well. When speed is important, set **facetres** to a low value. When the display is important, increase the **facetres** setting.

The user reference manual doesn't mention that **facetres** affects rendering, but it definitely does.

**Default:** 0.5

**Saved in:** Drawing file

# Fflimit (Release 13 and up)

**Advantage:** When set properly, this system variable can keep too many TrueType and PostScript fonts from clogging up your memory.

**Function:** By default, AutoCAD will be more than happy to

continuously load fonts into your valuable memory, which can
eventually slow down your productivity. By restricting the
value of **fflimit**, you'll force
AutoCAD to dump the fonts to
disk when you exceed the
limit. If you're consistently
bouncing in and out of text,
this solution is not good for
you because AutoCAD will
need to page out to disk to find
your fonts. If you're logically
creating your text all at one
time, this setup can be a great
memory saver! The **fflimit**
default of 0, instructs Auto-
CAD that there is no limit. I
suggest a small value of 2 or 3.
**Default:** 0 (no limit)
**Saved in:** Configuration file

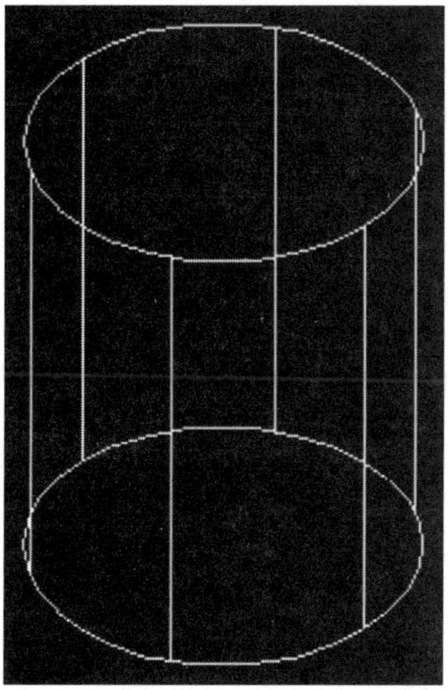

**Figure 4:** Isolines set to 6.

## Isavebak (Release 13 and up)

**Advantage:** Gets rid of those pesky backup files and helps
speed up saves.
**Function:** When set to 0, AutoCAD will not create BAK files.
Copying file data to backup files can dramatically increase the
time it takes to do a SAVE (especially in Windows). BAK files
also take up valuable storage space on your disk.
**Default:** 1 (Backup files created)
**Saved in:** Configuration file

## Isavepercent (Release 13 and up)

**Advantage:** Speeds up Saves.
**Function:** Convinces AutoCAD that it doesn't need to do a
complete SAVE every time you use a function that saves your
drawing. **Isavepercent** controls the amount of wasted space

within your drawing. To simplify this, let's say **isavepercent** is set to 50 (which conveniently happens to be the default). This setting means that AutoCAD will perform quick-and-dirty saves until 50 percent of your drawing is filled with wasted space. A quick-and-dirty save consists of tacking on new information and marking old information for designated changes. After reaching that 50 percent wasted space limit, AutoCAD performs a full save. A clean (full) save takes extra time because Auto-CAD does a total save, repacking, and removing any extra wasted space. You'll notice that a full save compresses your drawing file, thus making the file smaller than those quick-and-dirty saves. Setting the **isavepercent** variable to 0 turns this feature off altogether, thus, yielding only full saves.

**Default:** 50

**Saved in:** Configuration file

## Isolines (Release 13 and up)

**Advantage:** Improves the speed of regenerating 3D solids.
**Function:** Controls the number of tessellation lines that display on 3D solids. Tessellation lines help visualize a curved surface (cone, sphere, cylinder, and so on). You can't snap to isolines— they are for display only. The higher the number of tessellation lines, the slower regenerations will be and vice versa. Setting **isolines** to a value of 1 and turning **dispsilh** to 1 (on) can produce a simple display that regenerates quickly. When displaying splines, AutoCAD subtracts the number 4 from the value of **isolines** to determine the number of tessellation lines to display. For example, an **isolines** setting of 8 yields a total of four tessellation lines on the splined surface. This system variable is also intended to speed regenerations.

**Default:** 4

**Saved in:** Drawing file

## Maxactvp

**Advantage:** Can speed up regenerations in Paper Space.

**Function:** Controls the number of active viewports in Paper Space (when **tilemode** is set to 0). The lower the number, the faster the regenerations. An inactive viewport does not display its contents but will still be plotted.
**Default:** 16
**Saved in:** Not saved

## Maxsort

**Advantage:** This command allows you to tell AutoCAD to stop alphabetizing named objects, such as layers.
**Function:** Controls the number of named objects AutoCAD will sort alphabetically. If you prefer your layers to be listed within the layer dialog box in the order they were created, this system variable can help. Perhaps you'd like to list layers by priority, order of use, frequency, or some other criteria. Setting **maxsort** to 0 tells AutoCAD not to alphabetize any of your layers; they'll display in the order in which they were placed into the drawing. Caution: This variable controls all named objects including blocks, views, UCSs, and so on. You may have to weigh the advantages and disadvantages to your daily drawing routine.
**Default:** 200
**Saved in:** The configuration file

## Mirrtext

**Advantage:** Can be used to keep your text from mirroring when you use the MIRROR command.
**Function:** When selecting a group of objects to mirror, you might want any included text to be copied to the designated coordinate, but probably not mirrored. When **mirrtext** is set to a value of 0, AutoCAD will copy rather than mirror text when using the MIRROR command.
**Default:** 1 (too bad)
**Saved in:** The drawing file. Change your prototype drawing to

have a setting of 0 and you won't have to modify it for each individual drawing.

## Mtexted (Release 13 and up)

**Advantage:** Can be used to change the name of the text editor used to create and edit MTEXT.

**Function:** If you're a DOS user in Release 13, you probably won't like paging out to EDIT when you use the MTEXT command. You can supply your own favorite text editor or use the new single-line editor that comes with c4. The coding to use the new single-line editor is somewhat cryptic:

```
:lisped
```

(The colon isn't a typo, and the editor won't work without it.)
**Default:** Internal
**Saved in:** The configuration file.

## Pellipse (Release 13 and up)

**Advantage:** Allows you to create the polyline ellipses we've been using for years.

**Function:** With the new NURBS-based curves, we finally have true geometric ellipses starting with Release 13. To my surprise, several of my users need a way to create the old polyline ellipses. When **pellipse** is set to a value of 1, AutoCAD will draw the age-old ellipse made of many polyarc segments.
**Default:** 0 (creates the new ellipses)
**Saved in:** The drawing file.

## Plinegen

**Advantage:** Can be used to tell AutoCAD to consider an entire polyline when placing linetypes rather than between each individual vertex, as shown in Figure 5.
**Function:** When **plinegen** is set to a value of 1, AutoCAD will generate a linetype in a continuous pattern across all the

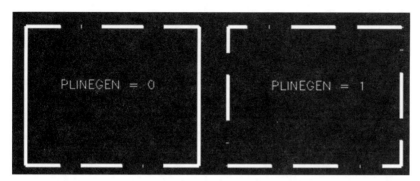

vertices of a polyline. When set to 0, AutoCAD will try to squeeze the linetype between the vertices—if there's enough room to do so. If you haven't been happy with the way your linetypes display on your polylines, this system variable should cheer you up!

**Default:** 0

**Saved in:** The drawing file.

## Plinewid

**Advantage:** Lets you quickly change the default polyline width before drawing polylines, which is especially useful with the RECTANGle command.

**Function:** Have you ever used the RECTANGle command only to find that a mysterious width had been used to create your rectangle? Where did this width come from? The width was stored from the last polyline drawn, and I'm sure you didn't intend to apply this width to your rectangle! To quickly set the width back to 0 (or any other setting), you can key in **plinewid** and assign a new value. Add it to a menu or button, and you won't have to type it in.

**Default:** 0

**Saved in:** The drawing file.

## Rasterpreview (Release 13 and up)

**Advantage:** Allows you to speed up your saving time.

**Function: Rasterpreview** is used to control the type of drawing preview file that is saved with the drawing. Every time AutoCAD executes the SAVE command, this preview file is recreated. As you're plugging along all day on the same drawing, the preview file isn't necessary. It's not really necessary until you exit the drawing. The CAD elders know that by setting **rasterpreview** to a value of 3, no preview image will be saved while you're saving. Before you leave the drawing, you can set it back to 0 to save a nice final bitmap of your drawing on your way out. The settings for **rasterpreview** are as shown here:

```
0 BMP file only
1 BMP and WMF file
2 WMF only
3 No preview image created
```

This variable is a must in a toolbar or menu. It's too long and too painful to key in every time you choose to modify its value. It is great combined with a high setting of **isavepercent** when you start a drawing (**rasterpreview = 3**). Then, before you finish your drawing, set **isavepercent** to 0 (to do a complete cleaning) and set **rasterpreview** back to 0.
**Default:** 0
**Saved in:** The drawing file.

**Figure 6:** SPLFRAME set to 1.

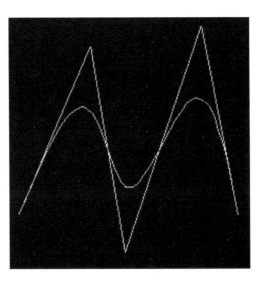

## Splframe

**Advantage:** Makes it easier to edit the new splines that came out in Release 13, shown in Figure 6.
**Function:** When set to a value of 1, **splframe** will display the control frame on SPLINEs. It will also

work on Polyline splines. When editing the new nurbs based SPLINEs, it's quite useful to see the control frame while you're in the SPLINEDIT command. Splframe will also display the invisible edges of 3Dfaces.

**Default:** 0

**Saved in:** The drawing file.

## Surftab1

**Advantage:** Permits greater control over the end results of the surface commands, RULESURF, TABSURF, REVSURF, and EDGESURF.

**Function:** If you're a 3D user, particularly Release 12, you may find these next two system variables particularly useful.

**Surftab1** controls the number of tabulations that are generated in RULESURF and TABSURF. If you want a smoother surface mesh, escalate the default value of 6 until you get the desired result. **Surftab1** also controls the number of 3Dfaces that are generated in the M direction for REVSURF and EDGESURF. The higher the value, the smoother the mesh.

**Default:** 6

**Saved in:** The drawing file.

## SURFTAB2

**Advantage:** Permits greater control over the end results of REVSURF and EDGESURF.

**Function:** REVSURF and EDGESURF have an M and N direction (3Dfaces going both ways). The **surftab2** system variable controls the number of 3Dfaces that appear in the N direction. The higher the value, the smoother the mesh.

**Default:** 6

**Saved in:** The drawing file.

## Textfill (Release 13 and up)

**Advantage:** Improves the look of TrueType fonts (and Adobe Type 1).

**Function:** When set to a value of 1, **textfill** will display text as filled characters. It takes affect after the first regeneration. Caution: It will slow you down, but it looks great!

**Default:** 0

**Saved in:** The drawing file.

## Textqlty (Release 13 and up)

**Advantage:** Can speed up regenerations and plotting of text.

**Function:** Sets the resolution of TrueType and Adobe Type 1 fonts. With a range of 0 to 100, 50 is the default. A setting of 50 defaults to a text resolution of 300 dots per inch. The highest value, 100, sets the text resolution to 600dpi and requires more time to regenerate and plot. A low setting, such as 25, would cause the text to appear more jagged but would speed up regeneration and plotting. If you're looking for speed, set the value far below the default value.

**Default:** 50 (300dpi)

**Saved in:** The drawing file.

## Ucsfollow

**Advantage:** Eliminates having to use the PLAN command whenever you change your UCS.

**Function:** When **ucsfollow** is set to a value of 1, AutoCAD will automatically generate a plan view whenever you change from one UCS to another. If you prefer to work on the plan view of your current construction plane, this system variable will prove invaluable. **Ucsfollow** is viewport dependent, so you aren't forced to use this setting in all viewports. **Ucsfollow** is saved separately for Paper Space and Model Space. Also, **Ucsfollow** is ignored when **tilemode** is set to 0 and you are working in Paper Space.

**Default:** 0 (off)

**Saved in:** The drawing file.

## Visretain

**Advantage:** Eliminates the tedious restructuring of layer settings each time you enter a drawing with external references.
**Function: Visretain** controls whether or not AutoCAD will save the modifications you've made to an external reference file's layers. When set to a value of 0, the default, AutoCAD discards any changes made to the visibility, color, or linetype of dependent layers. It can be very frustrating when you pull up the drawing at a future time to find your hard work has not been saved. Setting **visretain** to a value of 1 will force AutoCAD to remember if a dependent layer is on or off, frozen or thawed, or a particular color or linetype.
**Default:** 0 (change this value in your prototype file to 1 if you're an xref user).
**Saved in:** The drawing file.

Well, do you feel worthy of associating with the CAD elders now? These are just a few of the powerful system variables hidden within AutoCAD. Try these and others to fine-tune your AutoCAD skills. Remember, it's to your advantage to automate these variables as much as possible by assigning them to a toolbar or menu item. It's doubtful you'll want to key in these laborious command names. I hope you've found at least one system variable that will increase your productivity in AutoCAD.

# Index

# AUGI MEMBERSHIP FORM

Autodesk User Group International
P.O Box 3394, San Rafael, CA 94912-3394 * (415) 507-6145 fax
www.augi.com * www.eur.augi.com

| QUANTITY | DESCRIPTION | ANNUAL DUES | DUE |
|:---:|:---:|:---:|:---:|
| 1 | Annual AUGI Membership | $35.00 | $35.00 |

### *Please complete the following information:*

❏ New   ❏ Renew: Member # _____

Name _____
Email Address _____
Company Name _____
Address _____
City/District _____
State/Province _____
Zip or Postal Code _____
Country _____
Phone _____
Fax _____
Local User Group attended (if any) _____

**What is your company's primary business?**
❏ AEC                        ❏ Manufacturing/Auto
❏ Civil Engineering          ❏ Manufacturing/Elec.
❏ Education                   ❏ Transportation
❏ Electrical CAD             ❏ Utilities
❏ Facilities Management      ❏ Video/Film
❏ GIS                         ❏ Other _____
❏ Government

**What is your job function?**
❏ CAD/Data Management        ❏ Sales/Marketing
❏ Consulting                 ❏ Senior Management
❏ Designer/Engineer          ❏ Training
❏ Management                 ❏ Other _____

**How did you hear about AUGI?**
❏ Autodesk University        ❏ Magazine
❏ Dealer                     ❏ Work
❏ Friend                     ❏ World Wide Web
❏ Local User Group           ❏ Other _____

**Would you like to be an AUGI volunteer?**
❏ Yes!                       ❏ I'd like more information

**Industry Groups** (Please check all that you wish to join):
❏ AEC                        ❏ Mechanical
❏ Data Management            ❏ Multimedia
❏ Education/Training         ❏ Programming
❏ GIS

**Product information** (Please check all products that you use):
❏ 3D Studio MAX              ❏ AutoCAD R12
❏ 3D Studio VIZ              ❏ AutoCAD R13
❏ AutoCAD LT                 ❏ AutoCAD R14
❏ AutoCAD Map                ❏ Mechanical Desktop
❏ Designer                   ❏ Other _____

Please rate your ability on the Autodesk software you use:
Beginner ❏1 ❏2 ❏3 ❏4 ❏5 Expert

How many years have you been using Autodesk products? _____

What was the earliest product and release of Autodesk software
you have used? _____

How many Autodesk add-on products do you use? _____

How many 3rd party applications do you use? _____

How many people use Autodesk products in your workplace?
❏ 1–5  ❏ 6–10  ❏ 11–20  ❏ 21–50  ❏ 51–100  ❏ 100+

Do you have access to the Internet?    ❏Yes   ❏No

Does your company have Intranet?    ❏Yes   ❏No

How many people in your company belong to AUGI? _____

How many people do you share your AUGI resources with? _____

T-shirt size:
❏ M      ❏ L      ❏ XL      ❏ XXL      ❏ XXXL

Main reason for joining AUGI or renewing your membership?
❏ Career development         ❏ Telecourses
❏ Network worldwide          ❏ Web site
❏ Influence Autodesk         ❏ AU discount
❏ Learn about Autodesk products ❏ Newsletter
❏ Resource CD-ROM            ❏ I'm totally AUGI
❏ Other _____

AUGI membership runs yearly from receipt of the $35 member-
ship dues. Please send completed form and payment to **AUGI
MEMBERSHIP, P.O. Box 3394, San Rafael, CA 94912-3394**,
or FAX to **415-507-6145.** Allow 6-8 weeks for delivery of your
initial membership benefits package. For payment by credit
card, please complete the following information:

❏ American Express      ❏ Master Card      ❏ Visa

Signature _____
Credit Card # _____ Exp. _____

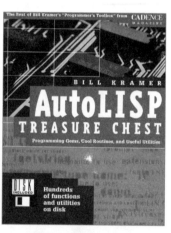

# Redesigned.
# Remodeled. Refined.
# Remarkable.

## CADENCE
### CHANNEL

Introducing CADENCE Channel, CADENCE magazine's newly redesigned Web resource for PC CAD professionals. Stay abreast of the trends, products, and people that are shaping the future of CAD with CADENCE Channel.

# Revisit www.cadence-mag.com